W9-DFW-384

THE CZECHOSLOVAK ECONOMY 1918–1980

Alice Teichova is Emiritus professor of Economic History at the School of Economic and Social Studies, University of East Anglia

In contrast to most other countries of Eastern Europe, Czechoslovakia has enjoyed an advanced level of industrialisation from a relatively early period. This together with its tradition of democracy has had a profound effect on her economic, social and cultural development. In this context the book outlines the history of the Czechoslovak economy which began to exist in 1918, was destroyed between 1938 and 1945, and restored after 1945. It assesses social and economic change against the background of the international economy and the dramatic political events of the twentieth century — the break up of the Habsburg Monarchy, the Peace Treaty of Versailles, the Munich Agreement of 1938 and the dismemberment of Czechoslovakia, the occupation by Nazi Germany, the attempt to reconstruct a democratic Republic, the period of Stalinism and the 'Prague Spring' of 1968. Thus the book produces a balanced historical outline of the economy of Czechoslovakia between 1918 and 1980.

A volume in the Routledge series on the *Contemporary Economic History of Europe* edited by Derek Aldcroft.

CONTEMPORARY ECONOMIC HISTORY OF EUROPE SERIES
Edited by Derek Aldcroft

The Economy of Yugoslavia
Fred Singleton and Bernard Carter

The Economic Development of the USSR
Roger Munting

The Norwegian Economy
Fritz Hodne

The Spanish Economy
J.R. Harrison

The Polish Economy in the Twentieth Century
Zbigniew Landau and Jerzy Tomaszewski

The Hungarian Economy in the Twentieth Century
Ivan T. Berend and György Ránki

The Bulgarian Economy in the Twentieth Century
John R. Lampe

The Danish Economy in the Twentieth Century
Hans Christian Johansen

The Greek Economy in the Twentieth Century
A.F. Freris

The Romanian Economy in the Twentieth Century
David Twinock

The Czechoslovak Economy 1918-1980

ALICE TEICHOVA

R

ROUTLEDGE
London and New York

First published in 1988 by
Routledge
11 New Fetter Lane, London EC4P 4EE
Published in the USA by
Routledge
in association with Routledge, Chapman & Hall, Inc.
29 West 35th Street, New York NY 10001

© 1988 Alice Teichova

Printed in Great Britain by Billing & Sons Ltd, Worcester
All rights reserved. No part of this book may be
reprinted or reproduced or utilised in any form or
by any electronic, mechanical, or other means, now
known or hereafter invented, including photocopying
and recording, or in any information storage or
retrieval system, without permission in writing from
the publishers.

British Library Cataloguing in Publication Data

Teichova, Alice
    The Czechoslovak economy 1918–1980
    ——(Routledge series on the
contemporary economic history of Europe).
Translated from German by Richard J. Hockaday.
    1. Czechoslovakia——Economic conditions
    ——1918–1945
    2. Czechoslovakia——Economic conditions
    ——1945
    I. Title
    330.9437′03   HC270.27

ISBN 0–415–00376–8

Library of Congress Cataloging-in-Publication Data

ISBN 0–415–00376–8

ROBERT MANNING
⬜T   ⬜RARY

NOV 3 1988

Tallahassee, Florida

Contents

To Mutyo for his seventieth birthday

Abbreviations

BÚMF	Bankovní úřad ministerstva financí (Banking Office of the Ministry of Finance)
CCKSČ	Central Committee of the Communist Party of Czechoslovakia
CMEA	Council for Mutual Economic Assistance
Comecon	Council for Mutual Economic Assistance
ČSR	Czechoslovak Republic
ČSSR	Czechoslovak Socialist Republic
FRG	Federal Republic of Germany
GDR	German Democratic Republic
JZD	Jednotné zemědělské družstvo (Unified Agricultural Co-operative)
kč	Czechoslovak crown 1918–1939
kčs	Czechoslovak crown post-1945
KSČ	Komunistická strana Československa (Communist Party of Czechoslovakia)
NATO	North Atlantic Treaty Organisation
OECD	Organisation for Economic Co-operation and Development
ROH	Revoluční odborové hnutí (Revolutionary Trade Union Movement)
UNO	United Nations Organisation
UNRRA	United Nations Relief and Rehabilitation Administration
USA	United States of America
USSR	Union of Soviet Socialist Republics
VHJ	Vyrobní hospodářská jednotka (production economic unit)

Note: English translations of Czech and Slovak source references are given when they first occur.

Tables and Figures

FIGURES

Editor's Introduction

By comparison with the nineteenth century, the twentieth century has been very much more turbulent, both economically and politically. Two world wars and a great depression are sufficient to substantiate this claim without invoking the problems of more recent times. Yet despite these setbacks Europe's economic performance in the present century has been very much better than anything recorded in the historical past, thanks largely to the super-boom conditions following the post-Second World War reconstruction period. Thus in the period 1946–75, or 1950–73, the annual increase in total European gross national product *per capita* was 4.8 and 4.5 per cent respectively, as against a compound rate of just under 1 per cent in the nineteenth century (1800–1913) and the same during the troubled years between 1913 and 1950. As Bairoch points out, within a generation or so European *per capita* income rose slightly more than in the previous 150 years (1947–75 by 250 per cent, 1800–1948 by 225 per cent) and, on rough estimates for the half century before 1800 by about as much as in the preceding two centuries.[1]

The dynamic growth and relative stability of the 1950s and 1960s may, however, belie the natural order of things, as the events of the later 1970s and early 1980s demonstrate. Certainly it would seem unlikely that the European economy, or the world economy for that matter, will see a lasting return to the relatively stable conditions of the nineteenth century. No doubt the experience of the present century can easily lead to an exaggerated idea about the stability of the previous one. Nevertheless, one may justifiably claim that for much of the nineteenth century there was a degree of harmony in the economic development of the major powers and between the metropolitan economies and the periphery which has been noticeably absent since 1914. Indeed, one of the reasons for the apparent success of the gold standard since 1870, despite the aura of stability it allegedly shed, was the absence of serious external disturbances and imbalances in development among the major participating powers. As Triffin writes, 'the residual harmonization of national monetary and credit policies depended far less on *ex post* corrective action, requiring an extreme flexibility, downward as well as upward, of national price and wage levels, than on an *ex ante* avoidance of substantial disparities in cost competitiveness and the monetary policies that would allow them to develop'.[2]

Whatever the reasons for the absence of serious economic and political conflict, the fact remains that up to 1914 international development and political relations, though subject to strains of a minor nature from time to time, were never exposed to internal and external shocks of the magnitude experienced in the twentieth century. Not surprisingly therefore, the First World War rudely shattered the liberal tranquility of the later nineteenth and early twentieth centuries. At the time few people realised that it was going to be a lengthy war and, even more important, fewer still had any conception of the enormous impact it would have on economic and social relationships. Moreover, there was a general feeling, readily accepted in establishment circles, that following the period of hostilities it would be possible to resume where one had left off — in short, to recreate the conditions of the pre-war era.

For obvious reasons this was clearly an impossible task, though for nearly a decade statesmen strove to get back to what they regarded as 'normalcy', or the natural order of things. In itself this was one of the profound mistakes of the first post-war decade, since it should have been clear, even at that time, that the war and post-war clearing-up operations had undermined Europe's former equipoise and sapped her strength to a point where the economic system had become very sensitive to external shocks. The map of Europe had been rewritten under the political settlements following the war and this further weakened the economic viability of the continent and left a dangerous political vacuum in its wake. Moreover, it was not only in the economic sphere that Europe's strength had been reduced; in political and social terms the European continent was seriously weakened and many countries in the early post-war years were in a state of social ferment and upheaval.[3]

Generally speaking, Europe's economic and political fragility was ignored in the 1920s, probably more out of ignorance than intent. In their efforts to resurrect the pre-war system statesmen believed they were providing a viable solution to the problems of the day, and the fact that Europe shared in the prosperity of the later 1920s seemed to vindicate their judgement. But the post-war problems — war debts, external imbalances, currency issues, structural distortions and the like — defied solutions along traditional lines. The most notable of these was the attempt to restore a semblance of the gold standard in the belief that it had been responsible for the former stability. The upshot was a set of haphazard and inconsistent currency stabilisation policies which took no account of the changes in relative costs and prices among countries since 1914. Consequently, despite the apparent prosperity of the latter half of the decade, Europe remained in a state of unstable equilibrium and therefore vulnerable to any external shocks. The collapse of US foreign lending from the middle of 1928 and the subsequent downturn of the American economy a year later exposed the weaknesses of the European economy. The structural supports were too weak to withstand violent shocks and so the edifice disintegrated.

That the years 1929–32/3 experienced one of the worst depressions and financial crises in history is not altogether surprising given the convergence of many unfavourable forces at that point in time. Moreover, the fact that a cyclical downturn occurred against the backdrop of structural disequilibrium only served to exacerbate the problem, while the inherent weakness of certain financial institutions in Europe and the United States led to extreme instability. The intensity of the crisis varied a great deal, but few countries, apart from the USSR, were unaffected. The action of governments tended to aggravate rather than ease the situation. Such policies included expenditure cuts, monetary contraction, the abandonment of the gold standard and protective measures designed to insulate domestic economies from external events. In effect these policies, while sometimes affording temporary relief to hard-pressed countries, in the end led to income destruction rather than income creation. When recovery finally set in in the winter of 1932/3 it owed little to policy contributions, though subsequently some Western governments did attempt more ambitious programmes of stimulation, while many of the poorer Eastern European countries adopted autarchic policies in an effort to push forward industrialisation. Apart from some notable exceptions, Germany and Sweden in particular, recovery from the slump, especially in terms of employment generation, was slow and patchy and even at the peak of the upswing in 1937 many countries were still operating below their resource capacity. A combination of weak real growth forces and structural imbalances in development would no doubt have ensured a continuation of resource under-utilisation had not rearmament and the outbreak of war served to close the gap.

Thus, by the eve of the Second World War Europe as a whole was in a much weaker state economically than it had been in 1914, with her shares of world income and trade notably reduced. Worse still, she emerged from the war in 1945 in a more prostrate condition than in 1918, with output levels well down on those of pre-war. In terms of the loss of life, physical destruction and decline in living standards Europe's position was much worse than after the First World War. On the other hand, recovery from wartime destruction was stronger and more secure than in the previous case. In part this can be attributed to the fact that in the reconstruction phase of the later 1940s some of the mistakes and blunders of the earlier experience were avoided. Inflation, for example, was contained more readily between 1939 and 1945 and the violent inflations of the early 1920s were not for the most part perpetuated after the Second World War. With the exception of Berlin, the map of Europe was divided much more cleanly and neatly than after 1918. Though it resulted in two ideological power blocs, the East and the West, it did nevertheless dispose of the power vacuum in Central/East Europe which had been a source of friction and contention in the interwar years. Moreover, the fact that each bloc was dominated or backed by a wealthy and rival superpower meant that support was forthcoming for the satellite countries. The vanquished powers were not, with the exception of East Germany, burdened by unreasonable exactions which had been the cause of so much bitterness and squabbling during the 1920s. Finally, governments no longer hankered after the 'halcyon' pre-war days, not surprisingly given the rugged conditions of the 1930s. This time it was to be planning for the future which occupied their attention, and which found expression in the commitment to maintain full employment and all that that entailed in terms of growth and stability, together with a conscious desire to build upon the earlier social welfare foundations. In wider perspective, the new initiatives found positive expression in terms of a readiness to co-operate internationally, particularly in trade and monetary matters. The liberal American aid programme for the West in the later 1940s was a concrete manifestation of this new approach.

Thus despite the enormity of the reconstruction task facing Europe at the end of the war, the recovery effort, after some initial difficulties, was both strong and sustained, and by the early 1950s Europe had reached a point where she could look to the future with some confidence. During the next two decades or so virtually every European country, in keeping with the buoyant conditions in the world economy as a whole, expanded very much more rapidly than in the past. This was the super-growth phase during which Europe regained a large part of the relative losses incurred between 1914 and 1945. The Eastern bloc countries forged ahead the most rapidly under their planned regimes, while the Western democracies achieved their success under mixed enterprise systems with varying degrees of market freedom. In both cases the state played a far more important role than hitherto, and neither system could be said to be without its problems. The planning mechanism in Eastern Europe never functioned as smoothly as originally anticipated by its proponents, and in due course most of the socialist countries were forced to make modifications to their systems of control. Similarly, the semi-market systems of the West did not always produce the right results so that governments were obliged to intervene to an increasing extent. One of the major problems encountered by the demand-managed economies of the West was that of trying to achieve a series of basically incompatible objectives simultaneously — namely full employment, price stability, growth and stability and external equilibrium. Given the limited policy weapons available to governments, this proved an impossible task to accomplish in most cases, though West Germany managed to achieve the seemingly impossible for much of the period.

Although these incompatible objectives proved elusive *in toto*, there was, throughout most of the period to the early 1970s, little cause for serious alarm. It is true that there were minor lapses from full employment; fluctuations still occurred but they were very moderate and took the form of growth cycles; some countries experienced periodic balance of payments problems; while prices generally rose continuously though at fairly modest annual rates. But such lapses could readily be accommodated, even with the limited policy choices, within an economic system that was growing rapidly. And there was some consolation from the fact that the planned socialist economies were not immune from some of these problems, especially later on in the period. By the later 1960s, despite some warning signs that conditions might be deteriorating, it seemed that Europe had entered a phase of perpetual prosperity not dissimilar to the one the Americans had conceived in the 1920s. Unfortunately, as in the earlier case, this illusion was to be rudely shattered in the first half of the 1970s. The super-growth phase of the post-war period culminated in the some-what feverish and speculative boom of 1972–3. By the following year the growth trend had been reversed, the old business cycle had reappeared and most countries were experiencing inflation at higher rates than at any time in the past half century. From that time onwards, according to Samuel Brittan, 'everything seems to have gone sour and we have had slower growth, rising unemployment, faster inflation, creeping trade restrictions and all the symptoms of stagflation'.[4] In fact, compared with the relatively placid and successful decades of the 1950s and 1960s, the later 1970s and early 1980s have been extremely turbulent, reminiscent in some respects of the interwar years.

It should of course be stressed that by comparison with the interwar years or even with the nineteenth century, economic growth has been quite respectable since the sharp boom and contraction in the first half of the 1970s. It only appears poor in relation to the rapid growth between 1950 and 1973 and the question arises as to whether this period should be regarded as somewhat abnormal with the shift to a lower growth profile in the 1970s being the inevitable consequence of long-term forces involving some reversal of the special growth promoting factors of the previous decades. In effect this would imply some weakening of real growth forces in the 1970s which was aggra-vated by specific factors, for example energy crises and policy variables.

The most disturbing feature of this later period was not simply that growth slowed down but that it became more erratic, with longer recessionary periods involving absolute contractions in output, and that it was accompanied by mount-ing unemployment and high inflation. Traditional Keynesian demand management policies were unable to cope with these problems and, in an effort to deal with them, particularly in-flation, governments resorted to ultra-defensive policies and monetary control. These were not very successful either, since the need for social and political compromise in policy-making meant that they were not applied rigorously enough to eradicate inflation, yet at the same time their influence was sufficiently strong to dampen the rate of growth thereby exacerbating unemployment. In other words, economic management is faced with an awkward policy dilemma in the prevailing situation of high unemployment and rapid inflation. Policy action to deal with either one tends to make the other worse, while the constraint of the political consensus produces an uneasy compromise in an effort to 'minimise macroeconomic misery'.[5] Rostow has neatly summarised the constraints involved in this context: 'Taxes, public expenditure, interest rates, and the supply of money are not determined antiseptically by men free to move economies along a Phillips curve to an optimum trade-off between the rate of unemployment and the rate of inflation. Fiscal and monetary policy are, inevitably, living parts of the democratic political process.'[6]

Whether the current problems of contemporary Western capitalism or the difficulties associated with the planning mechanisms of the socialist countries of Eastern Europe are amenable to solutions remains to be seen. It is not, for the most part, the purpose of the volumes in this series to speculate about the future. The series is designed to provide clear and balanced surveys of the economic development and problems of individual European countries from the end of the First World War through to the present, against the background of the general economic and political trends of the time. Though most European countries have shared a common experience for much of the period, it is none the less true that there has been considerable variation among countries in the rate of development and the manner in which they have sought to regulate and control their economies. The problems encountered have also varied widely, in part reflecting disparities in levels of development. While most European countries had, by the end of the First World War, achieved some industrialisation and made the initial breakthrough into modern economic growth, nevertheless there existed a wide gulf between the richer and poorer nations. At the beginning of the period the most advanced region was North-west Europe including Scandinavia and as one moved east and south so the level of *per capita* income relative to the European average declined. In some cases, notably Bulgaria, Yugoslavia and Portugal, income levels were barely half the European average. The gap has narrowed over time but the general pattern remains basically the same. Between 1913 and 1973 most of the poorer countries in the east and south (apart from Spain) raised their real *per capita* income levels relative to the European average, with most of the improvement taking place after 1950. Even so, by 1973 most of them, with the exception of Czechoslovakia, still fell below the European average, ranging from 9 to 15 per cent in the case of the USSR, Hungary, Greece, Bulgaria and Poland, to as much as 35–45 per cent for Spain, Portugal, Romania and Yugoslavia. Italy and Ireland also recorded *per capita* income levels some way below the European average.[7]

The present volume in the *Contemporary Economic History of Europe* appears at an appropriate time, to mark the seventieth anniversary of the origin of the Republic of Czechoslovakia. Like many other Eastern bloc countries it has had a chequered history since the First World War but at least it started life in a somewhat stronger position economically than that of her Eastern neighbours, with an industrial and agrarian structure more akin to that of Western Europe. Not that this shielded her from the ravages of the Great Depression and the Second World War. Indeed, Czechoslovakia suffered badly in the 1929–33 crisis partly because of the failure to restructure and modernise her economy. The result was that it became one of the most tightly controlled capitalist economies in interwar Europe with a high degree of cartelisation.

Though the Second World War produced greater distortions than the Great War, recovery was faster after 1945 than in the previous case. The subsequent growth of the economy replicated the high achievement of the Eastern bloc countries in the post-war period, though with the inevitable lag in agriculture and wages. But as Professor Teichova points out in her fascinating study, Czechoslovakia had certain features which were in some respects unique. For example, nationalisation or state ownership went further than in any other Central or Southeast European country, while Czechoslovakia became the most egalitarian of all the planned economies. Such characteristics raised difficulties in terms of growth and distribution of investment resources, not least in the more troubled times of the recent past when some of the problems of Western capitalism have emerged in the planned economies. Whether they are more adept at solving these than the West remains to be seen.

Derek Aldcroft

NOTES

1. P. Bairoch, 'Europe's gross national product: 1800–1975', *Journal of European Economic History*, no. 5 (Fall 1976), pp. 298–9.

2. R. Triffin, *Our international monetary system: yesterday, today and tomorrow*, New York, 1968, p. 14; see also D.H. Aldcroft, *From Versailles to Wall Street, 1919–1929,* London, 1977, pp. 162–4. Some of the costs of the gold standard system may, however, have been borne by the countries of the periphery, for example the Latin American.

3. See P. N. Stearns, *European society in upheaval*, New York, 1967.

4. *Financial Times*, 14 February 1980.

5. J.O.N. Perkins, *The macroeconomic mix to stop stagflation*, London, 1980.

6. W.W. Rostow, *Getting from here to there*, London, 1979.

7. See Bairoch, 'Europe's gross national product', pp. 297, 307.

Introduction

This book has been on my mind ever since 1968 when, after having lived in Prague for 20 years, I left Czechoslovakia, the country which I adopted, or rather which adopted me, by marriage to a citizen of it. On returning to Britain I became increasingly aware of how little is known in the West of this country's people, its history and economy. Only for a few brief but highly dramatic events its fate caught the imagination of the world and, indeed, triggered off significant historic changes.

In 1348 the University of Prague, known as Charles University was founded as the first university in Central Europe. On 23 May 1618 the famous defenestration took place in the Prague Castle. It started the rising of the Czech estates against the Habsburgs and marked the beginning of the Thirty Years War, The result was the end of the independent Czech state for 300 years. In 1848 Czech national aspirations received a severe blow when the revolution in Central Europe suffered its first military defeat with the crushing of the Prague uprising. In 1918, the end of the First World War brought the Czechs and Slovaks a formally independent democratic state with the establishment of the First Czechoslovak Republic on 28 October. It was this state, the only surviving parliamentary democracy in Central and South-east Europe on the eve of the Second World War, which Neville Chamberlain referred to as a 'far away country' inhabited by 'people of whom we know nothing'. Its independence was signed away by its Western allies 50 years ago, on 30 September 1938 in Munich.

Re-emerging as an independent republic after the years of brutal occupation by National Socialist Germany, Czechoslovakia attempted to combine socialism and democracy, which aroused expectations during the reconstruction period from 1945 to 1948. But the policy was reversed under the influence of Stalinism. Hopes for 'socialism with a human face' rose during the Prague Spring of 1968, but had to be tragically abandoned when Czechoslovakia's Eastern allies put a stop to the reforms, many features of which they are themselves trying to realise 20 years after.

It is difficult to understand these events which left their mark without realising that they are an integral part of the history of Czechoslovakia: the tradition of religious tolerance and democracy, the advanced level of industrialisation of its economy, and the high level of its intellectual and cultural climate.

When the series editor, Professor Derek Aldcroft, invited me to write an economic history of Czechoslovakia I was delighted to accept. I saw in this an opportunity to thank the historians of Czechoslovakia with whom I had the privilege and pleasure to work at Charles University and from whom I learned to appreciate the history of their country.

Although the first draft of the manuscript covering the inter-war period was written in English in the early 1970s, I prepared the whole text in the second half of the 1970s in German. A short version is published as a chapter in Wolfram Fischer (ed.), *Europäische Wirtschafts- und Sozialgeschichte*, vol. 6. At this point I wish to thank the publisher Klett-Cotta for permission to draw on material in this chapter. After spending some more time researching mainly into the post-1945 period I completed the work on the manuscript in 1984. I am greatly indebted to Richard J. Hockaday, who translated the entire text from German into English, and I wish to thank him most warmly for the suggestions he made to improve its readability.

I should like to express my thanks to the institutions which have provided financial aid to further my research in East European economic history since I took up academic work in Britain in 1969. They are the former Social Science Research Council, the British Academy and the Volkswagen Foundation. During research projects funded by those organisations I was able to collect material relevant to writing the economic history of Czechoslovakia.

The manuscript was read by Professors Wolfram Fischer of the Free University in Berlin, Arnošt Klíma of Charles University in Prague and Alois Mosser of the University of Vienna, by Dr Mikuláš Teich, Emeritus Fellow of Robinson College, Cambridge, and by Professor Derek Aldcroft, the series editor. I thank them for their helpful comments. The views expressed, however, are my own and for any errors and omissions I must take personal responsibility.

I hope that this outline of the economic history of Czechoslovakia since its establishment as an independent state in 1918 to 1980, which is to appear in 1988, the seventieth anniversary of the republic's origin, will contribute to a better understanding of the part the country played in recent history.

Alice Teichova

Part 1

Czechoslovakia, 1918–45

1

Population

STRUCTURE AND GROWTH

According to the first census carried out in the newly formed Republic of Czechoslovakia (ČSR) in 1921, the state had a population of 13,612,424 and covered an area of 140,519 square kilometres. For the development of an independent economy within the boundaries of this Successor State, it was of major significance that, despite only encompassing a fifth of the total area and a quarter of the inhabitants of the former Habsburg monarchy, it contained much more than half of Austria-Hungary's industrial potential and just under half of the workers who had been employed in the empire's industry.

Between 1921 and 1937, the last complete year in the statistical series of the First Republic, the population grew from 13.6 to 15.2 million. This population growth had differing effects on the four national parts of the state (see Table 1.1). The western part — the Czech part (also known as the Historical Lands) — was made up of *Bohemia*, which covered 37 per cent of the area of the entire nation with a population that fell from 49 per cent in 1921 to 47.5 per cent in 1937, and *Moravia and Silesia* which spread over some 19 per cent and the population of which dropped slightly from 24.5 per cent to 24 per cent. *Slovakia* took in an area of 35 per cent and the number of its inhabitants increased from 22 per cent to 23.2 per cent. The eastern part of the republic, *Carpatho-Ukraine*, covered 9 per cent of the total area and its population grew from 4.5 per cent to 5.3 per cent. The general fall in the growth rate from 10.96 to 3.94 per 1,000 inhabitants shown in Table 1.2 reflected the overall European trend, whereby the natural growth-rate

Table 1.1: Area and population of Czechoslovakia, 1921–80

Country	Area				Population							
	1921	1950	1921	1950	ČSR 1921		1937		ČSSR 1950		1980	
	1,000 km²	1,000 km²	in %	in %	in 1,000	in %	in 1,000	in %	in 1,000	in %	in 1,000	in %
Bohemia	52.1	52.1	37	41	6,671	49	7,248	48 }	8,896 }	72	10,331	68
Moravia-Silesia	26.8	26.8	19	21	3,339	25	3,640	24 }				
Slovakia	49.0	49.0	35	38	2,998	22	3,540	23	3,442	28	4,952	32
Carpatho-Ukraine[1]	12.7		9		605	4	809	5				
Total	140.6	127.9	100	100	13,613	100	15,237	100	12,338	100	15,283	100

[1] Until 1938 Subcarpathian Russia (Ruthenia).

Sources: Censuses of the State Statistical Office in Prague, 1921 and 1950: *Vývoj společnosti v číslech* (Social development in numbers) (Prague, 1965); relevant years of *Statistická ročenka ČSR* and *Československá statistika* (Statistical Yearbook ČSR and Czechoslovak Statistics) (official publication of the state, later Federal Statistical Office).

Table 1.2: Population growth in Czechoslovakia, 1921/5–1975/9 (in %)

Country	ČSR		ČSSR				
	1921/5	1937	1945/9	1950/54	1955/9	1965/9	1975/9
Bohemia	7.5	0.3 ⎫					
Moravia-Silesia	10.9	4.0 ⎬	7.8	8.6	5.9	3.1	5.5
Slovakia	16.4	8.6	11.3	17.5	16.2	9.6	10.9
Carpatho-Ukraine	21.7	61.4					
Total	11.0	3.9	8.8	11.1	8.8	5.1	7.3

Sources: *Statistická ročenka* (1941), p. 147; *25 let Československa*, (25 years Czechoslovakia) (Prague, 1970), p. 251; *Československá statistika* (relevant years).

increased relatively in percentage terms from north-west to south-east. However, the rate of population growth in Czechoslovakia differed from the overall pattern in that its rate of increase of 11 per cent during the interwar years was far below the European average of approximately 20 per cent, whereas the increase in the population of the South-east European nations was significantly above this average.

MIGRATION

As a result of the relatively unfavourable demographic development in Czechoslovakia, the average age of the population between the two world wars rose from approximately 23 to 27. The main factors in this were the lower birth rate — despite a drop in child mortality from 156 in 1921–5 to 121 per 1,000 births in 1937 — and a simultaneous increase in the life expectancy of the age group from 45 to 64. In addition, people continued to emigrate in search of better economic and social conditions. This stream of emigrants which had started around the turn of the century was only slowed significantly by the slump and the associated immigration prohibitions, particularly to the Unites States of America. Almost half a million inhabitants of Czechoslovakia, in the main from Slovakia and the poorest agricultural regions of the Czech Lands, emigrated to North and South America, France and Germany in the years between 1920 and 1937. Over the same period of time, some

5

260,000 people — of whom 220,000 came from Slovakia — left their homes as seasonal workers, mostly in West Europe.

In Czechoslovakia itself, unskilled workers wandered westwards to the Czech Lands in search of a livelihood, while the Czechs moved to Slovakia and the Carpatho-Ukraine as civil servants, transport officials, army officers, teachers, office employees and all types of specialists.

The growth of the towns and cities developed hand in hand with advancing industrialisation. In the Czech Lands, growth was in line with the European average, whereas Slovakia lagged some 40 years behind. As late as 1930, 52.6 per cent of the population lived in communities with less than 2,000 inhabitants. Close bonds of kinship continued to exist between the rural and urban populations. Only five municipalities could count in excess of 100,000 inhabitants. Of these, Prague, the capital of the republic, was the biggest with 848,823 people; Brno, the capital of Moravia, had 264,925 and Bratislava, the capital of Slovakia, 123,844. The two largest industrial towns, Plzeň with its famous brewery and the Škoda Works, Czechoslovakia's leading engineering and armaments concern, and Moravská Ostrava with its coal mines and iron and steel works numbered over 140,000 people. By comparison, only 26,675 people lived in Uzhorod, the capital of the Carpatho-Ukraine.

NATIONALITIES

The structure of nationalities in Czechoslovakia (see Table 1.3, classified according to mother tongue) is closely linked with the diverse historical, cultural and economic development of the individual parts of the country. After centuries of independent statehood, the Czechs in the Historical Lands were subjected to the rule of the Habsburg monarchy for a period of 300 years. Among them, groups of Germans had lived for centuries as an important minority. However, from the seventeenth century they shared the same nationality as the ruling elite. And after the collapse of the Central Powers in 1918 their self-confidence developed even further until the 1930s when they came to be used as an instrument for the disintegration of the Czechoslovak state. The Slovaks on the other hand had lived for a thousand years under Hungarian rule and had been subjected to constant pressure of Magyarisation. The two Slav peoples

Table 1.3: Structure of population in Czechoslovakia according to nationality, 1921–80 (in %)

Nationality	Population census of				
	1921	1930	1950	1961	1980
Czechoslovakia					
Czech	52.5	53.0	67.9	66.0	64.2
Slovak	15.1	16.4	26.3	27.9	30.5
Ukrainian and Russian	0.8	0.8	0.6	0.4	0.4
Polish	0.8	0.7	0.6	0.5	0.4
Hungarian	5.1	4.3	3.0	3.9	3.8
German	24.7	23.6	1.3	1.0	0.4
Others	1.0	1.2	0.3	0.3	0.3
	100.0	100.0	100.0	100.0	100.0
Czech Lands					
Czech	67.5	68.4	93.8	94.3	94.9
Slovak	0.2	0.4	2.9	2.9	3.3
Ukrainian and Russian	0.1	0.2	0.2	0.2	0.2
Polish	1.0	0.9	0.8	0.7	0.6
Hungarian	0.1	0.1	0.2	0.2	0.2
German	30.6	29.5	1.8	1.4	0.6
Others	0.5	0.5	0.3	0.3	0.2
	100.0	100.0	100.0	100.0	100.0
Slovakia					
Czech	2.4	3.7	1.2	1.1	1.1
Slovak	65.1	67.7	86.6	85.3	86.6
Ukrainian and Russian	3.0	2.9	1.4	0.9	0.8
Polish	0.2	0.2	0.1	0.0	0.1
Hungarian	21.7	17.6	10.3	12.4	11.2
German	4.8	4.7	0.1	0.1	0.1
Others	2.8	3.2	0.3	0.2	0.1
	100.0	100.0	100.0	100.0	100.0

Sources: *Vývoj společností ČSSR v číslech* (Prague, 1965), p. 90; *Statistická ročenka* (1981).

represented the majority of the inhabitants of the First Republic. With the Czechs as the economically, politically and culturally dominant nationality, followed by Slovaks and small minorities of Poles, Russians and Ukrainians, the Slav nationalities made up over 70 per cent of the total population. The remaining 30 per cent was composed of a large and economically influential German population and a not insignificant Hungarian minority. Although the German minority represented a fifth of the Czechoslovak population, there was no compact German-speaking region and they lived in groups of various sizes along the borders of Bohemia, Moravia and Silesia. In addition, they formed significant linguistic enclaves in central Moravia, in the capital cities of Prague and Bratislava, as well as in Slovakia. The Hungarians numbered less than 5 per cent and lived in south Slovakia as well as being scattered among the Ukrainians and Russians in the Carpatho-Ukraine, while the majority of Poles lived in the Těšín-Ostrava region.

In multinational Czechoslovakia, the minorities enjoyed incomparably greater democratic freedoms than other minority groups in the neighbouring Successor States. Nevertheless, economic and social life took on national overtones. In isolated cases, grievances were justified but, in the overwhelming majority of cases, national differences were exaggerated in the interests of competing political and financial groups, whereby the many cases of inconvenience and difficulties which the minorities actually suffered, despite the relatively liberal political atmosphere, were exploited for other ends.

DENSITY AND THE DISTRIBUTION OF EMPLOYMENT ACCORDING TO ECONOMIC SECTORS

Between 1921 and 1937, the density of the Czechoslovak population increased from 97 to 108 per square kilometre. According to the census of 1937, the population density ranged from 139 in Bohemia to 72 in Slovakia and 64 in the Carpatho-Ukraine (see Table 1.4).

Table 1.4: Density of population in Czechoslovakia, 1921–80 (inhabitants per square kilometre)

Country	ČSR		ČSSR		
	1921	1937	1950	1970	1980
Bohemia	128	139 ⎫	113	124	131
Moravia-Silesia	125	136 ⎭			
Slovakia	61	72	70	93	101
Carpatho-Ukraine	48	64			
Total	97	108	97	112	120

Sources: As for Table 1.1.

Table 1.5: Occupational distribution of population in Czechoslovakia, 1910–80 (in %)

Area	Year	Total	Agriculture, forestry and fisheries	Industry and trades	Other branches
Czechoslovakia	1910	100.0	42.0	34.1	23.9
	1921	100.0	39.6	33.8	26.6
	1930	100.0	34.7	34.9	30.4
	1950	100.0	30.9	36.3	32.8
	1961	100.0	22.5	46.9	30.6
	1980	100.0	13.1	55.2	31.7
Czech Lands	1910	100.0	34.4	39.9	26.7
	1921	100.0	31.6	40.0	28.4
	1930	100.0	25.6	41.4	33.0
	1950	100.0	30.6	39.6	29.8
	1961	100.0	19.1	50.3	30.6
	1980	100.0	12.6	55.9	31.5
Slovakia and	1910	100.0	63.5	17.4	19.1
Carpatho-Ukraine	1921	100.0	61.8	16.5	21.7
	1930	100.0	58.5	17.8	23.7
Slovakia	1950	100.0	53.5	25.2	21.3
	1961	100.0	32.3	36.8	30.9
	1980	100.0	17.9	51.4	30.7

Sources: *Statistická ročenka ČSR* (Prague, 1937, 1981); *Statistická příručka ČSR* IV (Statistical Handbook) (Prague, 1932); *Vývoj společnosti ČSSR v číslech* (Prague, 1965).

The distribution of employment in Czechoslovakia corresponded with the population density and this underlines the west–east gradient of development which is also revealed by other indicators. Despite the increasing attraction of industrial areas, far more than half of the active population of Slovakia and the Carpatho-Ukraine worked in agriculture, forestry and fisheries between 1921 and 1930. In contrast, the percentage of people working in the Czech Lands in this primary sector of the economy fell from 31.6 per cent in 1921 to 25.6 per cent in 1930. Although the figures in Table 1.5 showing the overall numbers employed in the three main sectors of the economy — agriculture and forestry, trade and industry and the service sector — give the impression of a balanced industrial agricultural economy, they also blur the regional and social-economic differences.

2

Society

SOCIAL CLASSES AND SOCIAL MOBILITY

The bourgeoisie

Following the collapse of the Habsburg monarchy and the post-war revolutionary wave which, in Czechoslovakia, developed into a national/democratic revolution, the nobility were displaced from their position as the leading political force by the Czechoslovak bourgeoisie. However, although aristocratic titles were abolished, the majority of these wealthy families retained their estates. Following the Battle of the White Mountain in 1620, the original Czech aristocracy was largely decimated during the seventeenth century and the Bohemian aristocracy which arose in the ensuing decades was descended from noble families in many different parts of Europe. Hence a distinct Czech aristocracy hardly existed in the early twentieth century. In Slovakia, the native aristocracy lost its ethnic identity and merged with the Hungarian nobility. An economically independent bourgeoisie had not developed fully, so that the peasantry formed the backbone of the Slovak nation. In distinction to the neighbouring states where traditional differences between the estates were maintained, a parliamentary democracy developed in Czechoslovakia. Under this system, all citizens were equal before the law. However, this by no means abolished the social differences which continued to exist within Czechoslovak society.

The upper bourgeoisie of the First Republic accounted for around 5 per cent of the population. However, it was no hermetically sealed group. Its members included the highest income groups — numbering some 22,000 families — with incomes, according to income statistics based on tax returns, ranging from 50,000 to 5,000,000 kč per annum stemming from the profits of large companies, as well as financial transactions, stock-exchange dealings, commercial activities and interest from securities. A handful of large landowners, known as the 'green aristocracy', were the recipients of Czechoslovakia's highest incomes amounting to almost 30 per cent of the total declared net agricultural profits. The bourgeois elite included influential statesmen and senior civil servants, leading personalities from the major political parties, as well as the academic professions, particularly university professors, physicians and lawyers who were held in high esteem by society at large.

The middle strata

One of the most numerous and highly differentiated social groups was the middle strata, which encompassed almost 20 per cent of the economically active population (5.6 million). In the main, it was made up of tradesmen, craftsmen, shopkeepers, specialists, small businessmen and dealers, white-collar workers and civil servants. Between 1921 and 1930, the middle strata shrunk by 3 per cent. Thereafter, this trend was intensified by the extended economic crisis of the 1930s.

Statistical inquiries have shown that the social mobility of this petty bourgeoisie was relatively great. There was a proletarianising trend among self-employed craftsmen such as tailors, shoemakers, smiths, joiners, etc. and their number fell during the interwar years. At the same time, there was an increase in the number of small entrepreneurs in the new branches of industry, such as electrical engineering, photography, motor-vehicle repairs, as well as services such as catering and cleaning. However, very few of them managed to develop their businesses sufficiently to join the ranks of the medium-sized enterprises and only a few isolated cases can be classified as having forced their way into the world of big business.

The numbers of white-collar workers and civil servants also increased. The social distance between this group and the working class was emphasised by new salary scales introduced in 1926. Above all, it was the senior civil servants who benefited from this move and, overall, the result was even greater social differentiation between civil servants and white-collar workers. Parallel to this, there was a continuation in the downward trend of the majority of white-collar workers into the working class, with 40 per cent of all white-collar workers drawing salaries which were comparable with the wages of skilled workmen.

Among the lowest income groups in the First Republic was a broad social layer made up of blue-collar employees and home workers. Salaried blue-collar employees, the majority of whom were employed in the transport, public health and school sectors, in the army and cultural institutions, as well as some private companies, belonged neither to the white-collar workers nor to the industrial workers. On the basis of their social attitudes, however, blue-collar employees must be ranked alongside the other middle-strata groups. Self-employed home workers also considered themselves to be a social cut above the working class and thought themselves to be more akin to entrepreneurs, because, despite the fact that in the majority of cases their income tended to be significantly lower than the average income of industrial workers, they used their own machines or tools to spend long working days processing the material of bigger companies. In the long term, it was difficult for these groups to avoid being caught up in the continuous process of proletarianisation.

The agricultural population

The overwhelming majority of the agricultural population consisted of small to medium-sized peasants. Between 1921 and 1930, their number grew as a result of the land reforms carried out during the 1920s with 64 per cent of all agricultural land being accounted for by holdings of 5–20 hectares. This amounted to 95 per cent of all agricultural holdings. During the same period, the number of agricultural and forestry workers dropped from 956,000 to 773,000. Accordingly, the greatest part of agricultural output was produced by the labour of the peasants and their families. Although there were only 16,135 farms with more than 50 hectares which, in turn, represented only 1 per cent of all agricultural enterprises, these larger farms covered some 20 per cent of Czechoslovakia's agricultural land. In the Czech Lands, these larger landowners belonged to the politically most influential group of the agricultural bourgeoisie.

At the bottom of the social ladder of the agricultural population, many peasants on small and dwarf holdings — particularly those in the eastern regions of the country — lost their property through indebtedness in the 1930s. Hence, they swelled the ranks of those without land or work and, in a process similar to that taking place in the South-east European countries, the pressures of relative overpopulation spread throughout Slovakia and the Carpatho-Ukraine because, due to the insufficient rate of industrial development, there was no possibility of the surplus being absorbed.

Although their numbers varied considerably, there was also ' a relatively large intermediate layer between peasants and workers consisting of part-time peasants — the so-called 'iron peasants' (*kovorolníci*) — who earned their livelihood by working in the nearby factories and tilling the land during their free time.

The workers

In Czechoslovakia, the social significance of the workers was comparable with that of the working class in neighbouring Austria and Germany and notably greater than in the South-east European countries. In 1930, there were some 2,040,500 wage-earners and, together with their families, they represented almost a third of the entire population. The overwhelming majority of the working class was concentrated in the industrial regions of the Czech Lands, particularly in the coal-mining, metal-processing, textile and building industries. Big companies employed over a third of all wage-earners, while approximately 40 per cent found work in smaller factories employing under 50 people. A quarter of all industrial workers were women. Young people aged up to 24 accounted for the relatively large proportion of 38 per cent of the entire work-force. About 300,000 people worked in private households as domestic servants.

In comparison with the period before the First World War, there was an improvement in the political and socio-economic situation of the working class. With its long tradition, the trade-union movement forms a certain indicator of this. During the revolutionary post-war years, the number of trade-union members increased rapidly and reached 1,979,700 in 1921. Soon afterwards, however, membership began to drop in stages. A major factor in this was the failure of the general strike of December 1920, as well as the movement's decentralised structure with eleven regional offices. In addition, the internal divisions according to political affiliations weakened the effectiveness of the trade unions, although they remained a significant force in the economic life of the republic.

A further indicator is formed by the annual average wage which, on the eve of the world economic crisis, was nine times higher than in 1913. However, this development conceals considerable differences within the working class. In 1928, the average wage in Bohemia was 8 per cent higher than in Moravia and 17 per cent higher than in Slovakia and the Carpatho-Ukraine. But the differences between the sexes were even greater with women earning on average 25 per cent less than men. In the clothing, textile, shoe and food-processing industries, however, female workers were paid an average of 40 per cent less than men doing the same jobs. Naturally, there were also differences between the individual branches of industry and, for example, the average wage of metal workers was twice as high as that received by brush-makers.

The social differences in general and in the working class in particular were not lessened during the 20 years' existence of the First Republic but worsened as, during the crisis years, unemployment rose between 1933 and 1935 to 30 per cent.

EDUCATION, SCHOOLING, MINORITIES

Czechoslovakia's education and schooling system reflected the democratic social system of the country and, in this field, the achievements of the First Republic could stand any comparison with its European neighbours. Czechoslovakia inherited a set of cultural circumstances which are best characterised by the west-east gradient of illiteracy extracted from the census of 1921 (see Table 2.1).

In the Cisleithanian part of the Habsburg monarchy, the origins of the modern system of education have their roots in the foundation of the 'Trivial' School by Maria Theresa in 1775. This was followed by compulsory school attendance for

Table 2.1: Percentage of illiteracy in Czechoslovakia, according to census of 1921

Areas	Percentage of illiteracy of all persons over 14 years of age
Bohemia	2.4
Moravia-Silesia	3.3
Slovakia	15.0
Carpatho-Ukraine	50.1

Sources: International Labour Office, Geneva; *The rural exodus in Czechoslovakia, results of investigations made by Dr H. Böker and F.W. von Bülow*, Geneva, 1935.

all 6- to 14-year-olds in 1869 and gave rise to the educational system with its stages ranging from elementary and middle schools to grammar schools (*gymnasium*) and universities. Following the turn of the century, illiteracy was almost completely banished from Bohemia and Austria, with the highest general level of education in Europe being reached in these areas. The Czechoslovak Republic was able to consolidate its comprehensive programme of education on this basis and carry out the most urgently needed reforms in the less advanced parts of the country. Accordingly, during the interwar years, a relatively balanced level of education in the individual school stages was attained throughout the entire republic.

At the beginning, the Czechoslovak government sent Czech teachers into Slovakia where, in 1918, there were only 390 Slovak teachers and 276 elementary schools for over 2 million people, and to the Carpatho-Ukraine where there were no schools at all. As the nationality policy of the republic took effect in the ensuing period, adequate funds were made available for educational facilities so that in 1930 practically all children of school age were being instructed in their native language (96 per cent Czechs, Slovaks and Romanians, 97 per cent Germans, 93 per cent Hungarians, 91 per cent Carpatho-Ukrainians and 88 per cent Poles). This educational policy covered both grammar schools with eight classes and secondary schools with seven classes, as well as the universities.

In common with the other European countries, there was also an increase in the number of universities in Czechoslovakia. After 1919 there was a ʹzech university in Brno, a Slovak university in Bratislava and a Ukrainian (*emigré*) university in Prague, in addition to the German and Czech university in Prague, the Charles University, which with a history stretching back to 1348 is the first Central European university. A rich tradition was also a characteristic of the technical universities which numbered among the first to be founded in Central Europe. There were two Czech and two German technical universities, one each in both Prague and Brno, an agricultural college in Brno and a mining academy in Přibram, a veterinary college in Brno and an academy of fine arts in Prague.

Students of oppressed minorities or members of persecuted religious communities from neighbouring countries could register at the Czechoslovak universities and technical universities and complete their academic studies there.

Within the framework of the Czechoslovak educational system, students could choose between going to four different types of vocational, trade, teacher training or agricultural colleges after completing their compulsory education. Thereafter, they had the chance of continuing their studies at the faculties of the universities, academy of art or technical universities.

There were religious and private schools, but the state educational system was predominant and the impact of this progressive cultural system on economic development cannot be underestimated.

3

The Economy

THE MAIN DIRECTIONS OF ECONOMIC DEVELOPMENT

A specific Czechoslovak market economy first came into being after 1918. Before this, the Czech Lands and Slovakia were integral parts of the economic structure of the Habsburg monarchy. Bohemia and Moravia had developed into the most advanced part of Austria-Hungary and the remaining, relatively backward territory of the Dual Monarchy represented a protected market for their industry. To the east, on the other hand, Slovakia entered the new state with an underdeveloped industry and the Carpatho-Ukraine, which became part of Czechoslovakia in 1919, ranked among the most underdeveloped parts of Transleithania.

Despite the regional socio-economic imbalances inherited from the monarchy, Czechoslovakia numbered among the highly industrialised countries of Europe. Faced by a diminished domestic market and the need to sell 30 to 40 per cent of the country's total production outside its borders, the Czechoslovak economy necessarily began to look for foreign markets. Contemporary economists considered the so-called Austro-Hungarian economic structure of Czechoslovakia as unhealthy and regarded the sole solution to the problem to be not in a complete restructuring of production, that is, to try to adapt the unfavourable structure to the new economic and political circumstances, but in a general export drive which should be supported by a corresponding customs and currency policy, as well as government subsidies. In certain post-war publications by economic historians, there is a widespread belief that the inherited economic structure did not change significantly during

17

Table 3.1: Indicators of economic growth in Czechoslovakia, 1919–37 (1929 = 100)

	1919	1920	1921	1922	1923	1924	1925	1926
Index of gross national product (GNP) (1913 = 65.7)[a]		59.4	64.2	62.5	67.7	74.4	83.5	83.2
Index *per capita* GNP (1913 = 69.1) in prices of 1929[a]		63.7	68.6	66.1	70.9	77.5	85.5	84.8
Index of industrial output[b]			60.1	54.7	57.6	76.0	79.0	76.7
Index of agricultural output[c]		79.9	80.2	91.0	91.9	92.7	98.2	90.9
Wholesale price index[b]				144.8	105.9	108.0	109.2	103.4
Wholesale price index of agricultural products[c]				141.0	101.6	109.1	109.0	103.5
Wholesale price index of industrial products and raw materials[c]				148.4	109.9	107.0	109.5	103.3
Living cost index[c]	75.3	128.8	137.0	116.0	90.0	93.2	97.0	96.0
Index of annual real wages[c]	51.0	69.2	85.5	89.8	93.6	92.1	89.0	91.0
Unemployment in thousands[c]	354.0	148.0	71.5	127.2	207.3	96.5	49.4	67.9
Number of strikers in thousands[c]	117.4	491.8	183.7	437.7	181.3	87.9	98.9	43.7
Export index (commodities)[d]		39.8	54.5	53.3	59.7	71.0	80.4	81.2
Import index (commodities)[d]		46.9	56.8	53.2	54.0	74.2	79.1	74.3

Sources: Compiled and where necessary recalculated from:
  (a) Frederic L. Pryor, Zora P. Pryor, Miloš Stádník and George J. Staller, 'Czechoslovak aggregate production in the interwar period', in *The Review of Income and Wealth*, 17/1 (1971), p. 364–8;
  (b) *Statistická ročenka Protektorátu Čechy a Morava*, 1941, pp. 185, 206;

1927	1928	1929	1930	1931	1932	1933	1934	1935	1936	1937
89.4	97.3	100.0	96.7	93.4	89.7	85.9	82.6	81.8	88.5	98.4
90.6	98.3	100.0	96.1	92.2	87.9	83.7	80.0	78.9	85.0	94.1
89.0	85.8	100.0	89.2	80.7	63.5	60.2	66.5	70.1	80.1	96.3
98.3	95.7	100.0	96.3	95.6	101.4	98.1	92.4	89.0	105.1	109.3
106.0	106.1	100.0	88.8	80.6	74.5	72.2	74.0	77.2	77.4	82.0
109.5	108.7	100.0	86.8	82.0	76.6	74.7	78.9	84.3	81.4	81.9
102.9	103.7	100.0	90.8	79.2	72.6	69.7	69.4	70.4	73.7	82.3
100.1	100.3	100.0	97.8	93.6	91.8	90.8	89.7	92.3	93.2	94.4
91.1	96.2	100.0	94.4	91.5	88.8	85.0	84.0	81.0	86.0	90.4
52.9	38.6	41.6	105.4	291.3	554.1	738.3	677.0	686.3	622.7	408.9
158.8	96.3	57.8	27.4	43.9	97.9	32.0	34.7	36.1	51.0	111.8
95.4	99.2	100.0	91.6	79.4	48.1	41.3	47.5	49.3	54.6	69.3
89.8	83.8	100.0	91.4	86.6	64.2	54.7	57.5	59.2	64.8	72.4

(c) Václav Průcha et al. (eds.), Hospodářské dějiny Československa v 19. a 20. století (The economic history of Czechoslovakia in the 19th and 20th centuries), Prague, 1974, pp. 503, 505;
(d) Zora P. Pryor, Frederic L. Pryor. 'Foreign trade and interwar Czechoslovak economic development, 1918–1938', Vierteljahrschrift für Sozial- und Wirtschaftsgeschichte, 62/4 (1975) p. 503.

the interwar years but that it actually became more pronounced and this, in conjunction with the loss of the Austro-Hungarian market, had a completely negative effect on the republic's rate of economic growth.

In the light of the results of new research, there can be no doubt that, in general, Czechoslovak entrepreneurs felt themselves to be under pressure from the competition of the advanced industrial nations, as well as the increasing industrialisation of the South-east European Successor States, and saw little choice other than adaptation and readjustment. However, this took place hesitantly and the slow pace of modernisation of industrial production in the first decade of success resulted in Czechoslovakia being forced by the world economic crisis (1929–33) into structural changes at a time of extremely depressed social and economic conditions. Because it was not possible to achieve a level of technical and organisational efficiency comparable with the most advanced industrial nations, the original, advantageous tendencies of development were lost and Czechoslovakia remained, with Austria, Finland, Italy and Norway, among the middle-ranking European industrial nations. According to the comparative statistics of the League of Nations, it belonged to the ten biggest manufacturers of industrial goods and to the seven largest suppliers of arms, as well as to those European countries most dependent on exports. Because of Czechoslovakia's great dependence on foreign trade and the international capital market, its economy was particularly vulnerable to fluctuations in the international economy.

There is a large number of calculations — based on diverse criteria and base years — illustrating the overall economic growth of the First Republic. Although the reliability of the data and results that diverge by some index or percentage points can be disputed, nevertheless, a basic trend regarding the essential features of economic development can be discerned in the statistics (see Table 3.1). The index of gross national product is based on calculations made by followers of Miloš Stádník, the founder of modern Czechoslovak national income accounting, which were published in 1971 and include figures from 1913 and 1920 to 1937. Table 3.2 shows the contributions made by the individual sectors of the economy to GNP in 1929: over a fifth came from the primary sector, almost half from the secondary sector and approximately a third from the tertiary sector. With the exception of insignificant movements, these

Table 3.2: Net domestic product by economic activity, 1930 and 1948–77 (in %)

Sector	Net Values			
	At factor costs		At current prices	
	1930	1948	1967	1977
Agriculture and forestry	22.8	19.0	11.1	8.3
Industry and trades	38.7	41.7	46.9	49.7
Building and industry	6.0	5.7	8.9	9.2
Transport	6.5	7.1		
Commerce, services and professions	11.9	12.2		
Housing	4.4	2.5	33.1	32.8
Banking, insurance and public service	9.7	11.8		
Total	100.0	100.0	100.0	100.0

Sources: Jaroslav Krejčí, 'Volkseinkommenvergleich Österreich-ČSR in *Beiträge zur Wirschaftspolitik und Wirtschaftswissenschaft II*, Schriftenreihe der Wiener Kammer für Arbeiter und Angestellte, (Vienna, n.d.) p. 19, for 1967 and 1977: Jaroslav Krejčí, *National income and outlay in Czechoslovakia, Poland and Yugoslavia* (London, 1982), p. 104.

Table 3.3: National income in Czechoslovakia by distributive shares (net in %)

	1930	1937	1948	1967	1977
1. Wages and salaries	43.8	43.5	52.9	46.4	47.5
2. Income from property and enterprises of self-employed persons — after 1948 including income of peasants in co-operatives	38.5	37.4	21.2	8.6	6.4
3. Undivided profits of companies — after 1948 state enterprises	5.7	6.4	7.4	45.0	46.1
4. Public income	12.0	12.7	18.5		
National income	100.0	100.0	100.0	100.0	100.0

Sources: Jaroslav Krejčí, 'Vývoj československého hospodářství v globální analýze' (The development of the Czechoslovak economy in global analysis) in *Politická ekonomie* (1968), 6, p. 589; Jaroslav Krejčí, *National income and outlay*, pp. 86–7, data for 1937 supplied by J. Krejčí.

proportions of the origin of Czechoslovakia's national product remained unchanged until 1938. In Table 3.3, the distribution of gross national income for 1930 and 1937 shows that in this case too there were no significant proportional changes because, at both times, over 40 per cent of national income comprised wages and salaries, including social insurance contributions, over 40 per cent of income came from property and the income of self-employed persons and co-operative farmers and approximately 12 per cent of revenue from property and concerns owned by the state.

Whereas the proportional distribution of national income remained constant, according to Jaroslav Krejčí's calculations, the volume in market prices in Czech crowns fell from kč 77.8 milliard in 1929 to kč 68.3 milliard in 1937, in other words, by 12 per cent. Of the individual groups, it was the incomes of the independent peasants that were most severely hit. Overall, they dropped from kč 16.6 milliard in 1929 to kč 9.8 milliard in 1937, that is by 40 per cent. Business profits fell by 22 per cent, the incomes of self-employed persons by 17 per cent, incomes from interest by 12.5 per cent and wages and salaries by a total of 8 per cent. During the same period, the incomes of *rentiers* rose by 195 per cent.

In comparison with other industrial countries where there was a relative drop, in Czechoslovakia, the proportion of incomes deriving from private property and independent enterprises remained at a significantly higher level. However, as a consequence of the political changes after 1945, it fell incomparably faster than anywhere else (see Part 2).

The development of the Czechoslovak economy, which can be seen from the indices in Table 3.1, is broadly comparable with the development of the international economy between the two world wars with certain deviations that were unique to Czechoslovakia.

The first phase coincides approximately with the first decade of the interwar years. In distinction to its neighbours, Czechoslovakia avoided the worst of the post-war confusion and, thanks to an early separation of the currencies coupled with a currency reform, the Czech crown (kč) was not caught up in the whirlwind of the Austrian hyper-inflation. Instead, the Czechoslovak government succeeded in stabilising the domestic currency and the economy despite a mild inflation. Between 1918 and 1920, the Bohemian and Moravian industries in particular absorbed the returning soldiers as they were demobilised and, because wages initially remained far below pre-war levels and prices rose rapidly (see Table 3.1), the basis for investment and, therefore, economic growth was laid. Despite the fact that, as in other Western industrial nations, gross national product and industrial production fell between 1921 and 1923, Czechoslovakia attained the pre-war levels in 1924 — the first of all the Successor States to do so — and exceeded them by a considerable margin in the following years.

All the harder for this was the impact of the world economic crisis on the Czechoslovak economy. The economic trends of the 1930s are similar to the French indicators and show the crisis first being felt in 1931 and continuing for a long time. By 1937, the overall economic levels of 1929 had not been reached again. Of all European countries, Czechoslovakia numbered among those nations that suffered the most severe drop in exports and industrial production and which were the slowest to recover. The rapid growth of the 1920s presents a sharp contrast to the deep and persistent crisis of the 1930s which in Czechoslovakia was intensified above all by a dramatic fall in exports in 1932 to a level two-thirds below that of 1929. In 1937, exports were still two-thirds of the 1929 level. Although the rate of growth of industrial production between 1929 and 1937 was relatively higher than that of exports, it still did not reach the level of 1929 before the dismemberment of the First Republic in 1938. On the other hand, agricultural production reacted typically to falling prices with increased yields (see Table 3.1).

Throughout the life of the First Czechoslovak Republic, real wages lagged behind the cost of living, as can be seen from Table 3.1 which also shows clearly how the number of unemployed fell to the lowest point (38,600) in 1928 but thereafter rose again to the high point of 738,000 in 1933 and remained alarmingly high through 1937. At the same time as unemployment increased by a factor of almost 20 the number of people on strike, with the exception of the turbulent months of 1932, dropped to the lowest level of the interwar years. This development was accompanied by greater productivity and, in conjuction with the structural changes brought about by the crisis, by greater orientation towards the domestic market. In the first decade of the interwar years, productivity rose in line with the growing level of investment. In the second decade, however, the productivity of the work-force continued to grow while the rate of increase in the level of investment declined. These contradictory developments came to the fore particularly during the economic crisis and under the pressure of unemployment.

AGRICULTURE, FORESTRY AND FISHERIES

The primary sector

In comparison with other European countries, Czechoslovakia ranked amongst those nations with an above-average area of agricultural land (42 per cent) and the greatest area of forest (33 per cent) as a share of total land area. Often wooded regions in remote eastern parts of the country prevented the efficient exploitation of the stands of timber. Accordingly, forestry did not reach the same high level as agriculture. Beside the general importance of the rich stand of coniferous and deciduous trees, forestry provided the raw materials for the domestic building, furniture and paper industries. Understandably, fishing played a basically insignificant role in this land-locked country. Mention should be made, however, of the fish farms, particularly carp breeding which has its roots in the Middle Ages. Altogether, carp ponds covered an area of almost 50,000 hectares, primarily in Bohemia (40,000 hectares).

In common with the other industrial societies, there was a decline in the number of people working in agriculture. Nevertheless, the primary sector continued to be of substantial economic significance.

The methods of cultivation employed in the fertile lands of Bohemia and Moravia belonged to the most intensive — even if they were not the technically most advanced — in Europe. At the same time, the methods of cultivation employed in many parts of Slovakia and even more so in the Carpatho-Ukraine were extensive and relatively primitive. Overall, the yield per hectare of Czechoslovak agricultural production remained above that of the European average, while the intensity fell steadily from west to east regardless of whether the standard applied was units of manpower or machinery to a given area of agricultural land or the yield quantity (see Table 3.4). The yield of industrial crops, which played a decisive role in the industrialisation of the Czech Lands, as well as in their export economy, was concentrated mainly in the north-west and south-west. In this connection, mention need only be made of the export of hops and sugar-beet — the 'white gold' of the country — the production of which greatly exceeded domestic requirements. Between 1926 and 1930, Czechoslovakia achieved the

Table 3.4: The west to east slope in agriculture in Czechoslovakia

(A) Proportion of agricultural population and agricultural labour on 100 hectares of arable land, 1921

	Bohemia	Moravia and Silesia	Slovakia	Carpatho-Ukraine
Number of agricultural population per 100 ha	56.4	64.4	59.3	63.1
Number of persons employed in agriculture	27.4	30.6	24.6	23.4

Source: E. Reich, *Základy organisace zemědělství ČSR* (Organisational principles of agriculture in the ČSR), Prague, 1934, p. 72.

(B) Average number of working days applied to 100 hectares of arable land annually, 1926–31

	Czech Lands	Slovakia and Carpatho-Ukraine
Annual number of working days per 100 hectares	122	102

(C) Average number of combustion engines and electrical motors applied to 100 hectares of arable land, annually, 1926–30

	Czech Lands	Slovakia and Carpatho-Ukraine
Number of motors per 100 hectares	6.2	0.6

Source: *Výrobní podmínky, organisace a výsledky zemědělských závodů v ČSR* (Production conditions, organisation and results of farms in the ČSR), Prague, 1935.

(D) Average output per hectare of arable land, 1926–31

Produce	Unit	Bohemia	Moravia and Silesia	Slovakia	Carpatho-Ukraine
Wheat	q	21.79	21.04	16.42	9.36
Rye	q	18.91	17.40	13.60	9.30
Oats	q	19.06	18.13	11.27	9.32
Potatoes	q	136.30	142.06	102.02	97.76
Beef	kg	76.10	64.10	34.10	37.30
Pork	kg	44.10	61.90	31.20	20.35

(D) Average output per hectare of arable land, 1926–31 (continued)

Produce	Unit	Bohemia	Moravia and Silesia	Slovakia	Carpatho-Ukraine
Milk	l	722.00	705.00	295.00	203.00
Poultry	kg	8.30	9.00	6.30	5.75

Source: R. Olšovský et al. (ed.), Přehled hospdářského vývoje Československa v letech 1918–1945, (Outline of the economic development in Czechoslovakia, 1918–1945), Prague, 1962, 2nd edn, p. 54.

(E) Average output of agricultural production in quintals per hectare of arable land, 1934–8

Produce	Czecho-slovakia	Europe without USSR	Germany	Austria	Poland	Hungary	France
Wheat	17.1	14.2	22.6	16.7	11.9	14.0	15.6
Rye	16.0	14.2	17.3	14.7	11.2	11.1	11.6
Barley	17.0	15.4	21.4	17.6	11.8	13.2	14.5
Oats	16.2	15.7	20.2	15.2	11.4	12.3	13.9
Potatoes	142[1]	135	169	137	121	73	112
Sugar Beet	286[1]	276	310	262	216	207	276

Note: [1] 1934–37.
Source: Jan Vachel, Postavení československého hospodářství ve světě v letech 1918–1965 (Situation of the Czechoslovak economy in the world 1918–1965), SKP-VŠE, Prague, October, 1967.

first place in terms of world production of hops, third place in sugar-beet and fourth place in potatoes. During the same period, Czechoslovak exports of hops, malt and sugar led the world with exports of the latter coming to an abrupt end with the collapse of the international sugar market in the world economic crisis. Until this time, the pre-war structure of agricultural production remained largely unchanged. However, the impact of the long agricultural crisis and increasing autarkic trends in Czechoslovakia's traditional markets brought about structural changes in which the production of export-oriented crops such as sugar-beet, barley and hops was cut back and the acreage of agricultural produce for the domestic market, that is, grain and potatoes, as well as animal husbandry, increased behind barriers of import duties.

When the Czechoslovak Republic first came into existence,

THE ECONOMY

almost one-third of all agricultural holdings farmed barely 3 per cent of the country's arable land while 0.5 per cent of all agricultural holdings disposed of almost one-fifth of arable land. According to the census conducted by the Czechoslovak Ministry of Agriculture for 1921, 14 of the biggest estates owned 11.3 per cent of all arable land and, even after the First World War, certain feudal economic conditions were still to be found. Among the rural population in Central Europe, there was a greater awareness of the conspicuous differences in land ownership, because the war had increased the political consciousness of the peasants and the Bolshevik Revolution had a major impact on their demands for a radical redistribution of the large estates. Hence, the rapid introduction of a land reform was acknowledged by both contemporaries and later observers to be a social, political and economic necessity for Czechoslovak agriculture. The land-reform legislation and its implementation was one of the most important acts carried out by the Czechoslovak government, which was forced into introducing and realising the reform programme by the fear of the revolutionary peasant movement and the intense hunger for land on the one hand, as well as by the necessity to support and extend capitalist

Table 3.5: Changes in land distribution in Czechoslovakia — number and sizes of farms according to the censuses of 1921, 1930 and 1955

Area	Number of farms in percentage of total			Percentage share of arable land		
Hectares	1921	1930	1955	1921	1930	1955
up to 1	31.9	30.42	46.10	2.9	2.61	4.58
1–5	41.7			20.1		
1–10		57.76	46.42		43.21	33.59
5–10	13.7			17.7		
10–50		11.21	5.87		37.15	16.15
10–30	10.8			30.4		
50–100		0.31	0.28		4.28	4.96
30–100	1.4			10.0		
100 and more	0.5	0.30	1.33	18.9	12.75	40.72
Total	100.0	100.0	100.0	100.0	100.0	100.0

Sources: *Mimořádné zprávy Státního úřadu statistického Republiky československé* (Supplementary bulletin of the State Statistical Office of the Czechoslovak Republic), Prague, 1931; *Postavení ČSR ve světovém hospodářství*, (Situation of ČSR in the world economy), Prague, 1957.

production and marketing methods in agriculture, in order to create better economic conditions for further industrial growth, on the other hand.

Land reform in Czechoslovakia was a long and complicated process. It consisted of three main laws: first, the Land Expropriation Law of 16 April 1919, which covered estates with more than 150 hectares under cultivation and over 250 hectares of non-arable land; secondly, the Land Allocation Law of 30 January 1920, which was to give priority to satisfying the demands of the peasants and then to divide the remaining land into 'residual estates' — estates of significant size averaging 80–100 hectares (however, the actual process was chiefly carried out in the reverse order); thirdly, the Compensation Law of 8 April 1920, which regulated the prices to be paid to the owners of the expropriated land. The reallocation of land on the basis of the Land Reform Law was practically completed by the end of the 1920s and the census of 1930 of the number and size of agricultural holdings showed that the economically efficient units — the medium-sized and larger holdings covering 5 to 100 hectares — were the decisive force in agriculture in Czechoslovakia between the wars (see Table 3.5).

The final results of the land reform of 1919 as published by the Czechoslovak Land Office at the end of 1937 show that the Land Expropriation Law took in 29 per cent of all land in Czechoslovakia (4 million hectares), of which 16 per cent was agricultural land (1.3 million hectares). However, 57 per cent of the expropriated land was returned to the original owners over the same period. A further 34 per cent was exempted from the expropriation so that the effective redistribution amounted to no more than 1,800,782 hectares. The most significant economic — and, accordingly, structurally most important — new element consisted of 2,291 'residual estates' which, with an average size of 100 hectares, covered 226,306 hectares (as a rule, 85 hectares were arable land), whereby, there was an increase in the number of agricultural holdings managed in accordance with the requirements of a capitalist market economy. The social and political aspects of the land reform are to be seen in the allocation of 789,803 hectares to 638,182 peasants, resulting in an average holding of approximately 1.2 hectares (of which generally 1 hectare was arable land). These dwarf holdings possessed insufficient means for efficiently utilising the land and, accordingly, the indebtedness of the peasants rose steadily. Many of these dwarf holdings were swallowed up during the economic crisis of 1929 to 1933.

On the one hand, the land reform created a larger number of new, small and medium-sized holdings. On the other hand, the last traces of feudalism vanished and the agricultural bourgeoisie was strengthened. Thus, favourable conditions were created for structural change in agriculture. Because of the close contacts with the co-operative movement, many of the characteristic features of structural change in Czechoslovakia were unique.

During the last decade of the nineteenth century, many different types of co-operatives were founded which, in a steadily increasing number, spread throughout the country, particularly in the Czech Lands. They varied from co-operative savings banks, buying and selling co-operatives and warehouses to market co-operatives for certain agricultural products, as well as co-operative sugar refineries, mills and distilleries. Diverse types of agricultural credit co-operatives played a major role during the Habsburg monarchy (their increasing membership can be seen in Table 3.6). They made a significant contribution to the development of domestic agrarian-finance capital by concentrating money which otherwise would have been widely scattered throughout the countryside. At the same time, through the provision of credit facilities, they ensured that small and medium-sized holdings — mainly of Czech peasants — enjoyed a fair degree of independence from the big Austrian banks and credit institutions.

Table 3.6: Number of Czech and German agricultural credit co-operatives in Bohemia, Moravia and Silesia, 1892–1916

Year	Number of co-operatives			Number of members		
	Czech	German	Total	Czech	German	Total
1892	12	50	62	–	–	–
1896	47	295	342	–	–	–
1900	663	684	1,347	68,400	56,600	125,000
1904	1,423	903	2,326	–	–	–
1908	2,098	996	3,094	–	–	–
1912	2,894	1,096	3,990	251,341	131,300	382,641
1916	2,971	1,123	4,094	–	–	–

Source: Raymond Polin and J.G. Charon, *Les Coopératives rurales en Tchécoslovaquie et en Roumanie et l'état*, Paris, 1934, p. 13.

The co-operative movement grew even faster after 1919 with the total number of co-operatives rising from 10,989 in 1919 to 15,946 in 1929. During the same period, the number of agricultural co-operatives increased from 2,373 to 4,100. Although not as powerful as the mighty industrial concerns, a dense network of co-operatives spread throughout Czechoslovakia, bringing together a large part of the agricultural production, the trade and the money of the economy.

In addition to being categorised on the basis of their products or specific functions, almost all agricultural co-operatives were organised in accordance with the nationality of their members. As their number grew, they formed federations which, until 1920, mainly concerned themselves with the provision of bookkeeping assistance. With time, however, each federation came to represent a certain category of co-operative and became the centre for the distribution of specific agricultural products and services (that is, corn, milk, animal husbandry or warehouses, machinery, credits, etc.). Their multifarious activities and their growth rate is shown in Table 3.7. Agricultural capital was concentrated in the centralised federative organs of the agricultural co-operatives and, in the course of time, they also came to control the granting of credits, the trade with agricultural products and the agricultural industry. By means of capital investments in the large public companies (joint-stock companies) of the chemical and armaments industry, the co-operatives became powerful partners of the industrialists and bankers and through their control over the agrarian party (Republikánská strana malorolnického lidu — Republican Smallholders' Party). Their representatives numbered among the country's leading politicians and they held important governmental posts (Ministries of Agriculture, Interior and Defence, as well as the Office of the Prime Minister).

The Czechoslovak agricultural co-operatives formed a central body at the initiative of the Ministry of Agriculture in 1921. By 1924, German and Slovak co-operatives had affiliated. With a membership encompassing some 90 per cent of all agricultural co-operatives, the 'Centrokooperativ' became the leading organisation. It was the accounting centre and also took central decisions in respect of market and credit conditions, as well as representing the Czechoslovak agricultural co-operatives at home and abroad. This advanced stage of development of the co-operative system led to an almost completely monopolistic

Table 3.7: Territorial distribution of non-credit agricultural co-operatives in Czechoslovakia

Kind of co-operative	Number of co-operatives				Number of members in 1930	Number of co-operatives in ČSR		
	Bohemia	Silesia	Slovakia	Carpatho-Ukraine/Ruthenia		1930	1937	1938
Warehouse	201	117	32	19	182,924	369	361	334
Grocery store	–	–	716	64	–	780	954	1,045
Dairy	137	291	67	9	75,568	504	521	524
Distillery	183	162	99	3	15,999	447	452	462
Flour mill and bakery	45	32	4	2	14,475	83	83	82
Vegetable	14	10	14	5	2,133	43	–	–
Chicory	32	–	–	–	5,111	32	32	32
Flax	16	10	–	–	2,548	26	32	33
Starch	7	3	–	–	881	10	8	12
Livestock sale	29	70	118	6	7,252	223	188	189
Seed	4	9	3	1	578	17	–	–
Fowl sale	5	–	1	–	461	6	–	–
Machine	141	57	7	–	7,276	205	184	173
Electric	1,912	183	5	–	111,467	2,100	2,031	2,034
Pasture	41	53	1	1	3,065	96	–	123
Forest	57	62	20	1	1,253	140	125	–
Vine	–	3	1	6	1,005	10	–	–
Brick	4	2	1	–	363	7	–	405
Miscellaneous	–	–	–	–	–	287	393	–
				Total		5,385	5,364	5,448

Source: L. Feierabend, *Agricultural co-operatives in Czechoslovakia* (New York, 1952), p. 98.

agricultural organisation which was formed with the aid of state subsidies during the early 1930s. In the main, it is the co-operative movement, its ability to organise the majority of the agricultural population (of the almost 15 million inhabitants of Czechoslovakia, some 6 million were associated with the co-operative movement), its tradition of gathering together the savings of the peasantry, as well as its monopolistic practices and its political power, which resulted in Czechoslovak agriculture being both more efficient and more concentrated than in any other Central and South-east European country.

The impact of the forces of concentration was not particularly great on the methods of cultivation. Instead, their main influence was on credit and finance conditions, market controls, product standardisation and regulation of the price and yield in agricultural production.

In the field of land cultivation, small and medium-sized peasant holdings dominated. When agricultural prices began to drop in 1928/9, Czechoslovak agriculture reacted with increased production in the 1930s (see Table 3.1). According to calculations made by the Agricultural Research Institute (Zemědělský ústav učetnicko-spravovědní), in the last year of the republic's existence, agricultural production was 10 per cent higher but the income of the peasants some 25 per cent lower than the average income during the second half of the 1920s.

Throughout the lifetime of the pre-Munich republic, Czechoslovak agriculture held its position among the most efficient countries of Europe. In comparison with other European countries, the yields were high (15 per cent *per capita* and 29 per cent per hectare above average), thanks to careful and competent soil cultivation and conscientious animal husbandry. However, in regard to the application of agricultural machines and artificial fertilisers, Czechoslovak agriculture stagnated at a level below that of the European average.

HANDICRAFTS, TRADE AND INDUSTRY

The secondary sector

During the interwar years, the importance of the secondary sector for Czechoslovakia's economy increased constantly. As

Table 3.8: Occupational distribution according to sectors of the Czechoslovak economy, 1921–80 (in %)

Year	Total	Agriculture and forestry	Industry and trades	Other branches, services
ČSR				
1921	100	39.6	33.8	26.6
1930	100	34.7	34.9	30.4
ČSSR				
1950	100	30.9	36.3	32.8
1961	100	22.5	46.9	30.6
1970	100	16.3	48.1	35.6
1980	100	13.1	55.2	31.7

Sources: *Vývoj společnosti v číslech*, p. 90; *Statistická ročenka ČSR* (Prague, 1937); *Statistická ročenka ČSSR* (Prague, 1981); *Statistická příručka ČSR* (Prague, 1932); *Československá statistika*, relevant years.

early as 1921, 33.8 per cent of the working population was employed in industrial occupations. This figure rose to 34.9 per cent in 1930 (see Table 3.8) and, at the end of the decade, although no further census was possible, there is no doubt about the growing share of the secondary sector in overall economic development. Realistic estimates indicate that, in 1938, the industrial sector accounted for 65 per cent of the total value of Czechoslovak production and that, in 1937, it contributed 35 per cent of the national income, 18 per cent of income tax and 47 per cent of profit tax.

Until 1929, the increase in Czechoslovakia's industrial production was greater than in the majority of European countries. If we take 100 as the average of the years 1925 to 1929, Czechoslovak industrial production is shown to have increased by 71.8 per cent in comparison with 1913: average growth in Europe, excluding the USSR, was 36.9 per cent; in Britain, it was 9.4 per cent; in Germany 17.3 per cent; in France 42.7 per cent; in Italy 81.1 per cent; in Belgium 40 per cent; in Holland 82.2 per cent; in Sweden 50.8 per cent; and in Austria 18 per cent. This fast economic growth was the direct consequence of increased capital investment and the resulting creation of efficient industrial capacity in the 1920s.

Czechoslovakia was the only country in Central and South-east Europe where industrial development resembled that of

West Europe, with the producer-goods industries being strengthened in relation to the consumer-goods industries. Although the share of the iron and steel, mechanical engineering and chemical industries in Czechoslovak industrial production lagged behind that of the West European countries, the rate of growth of the producer-goods industries in Czechoslovakia was higher than that of overall industrial production in these countries (see Table 3.9).

Table 3.9:
(A) Growth of industrial production in Czechoslovakia and in some other European countries, 1924–37 (1924 = 100)

State	Industry total	Mining	Metal- lurgy	Engin- eering	Chemical industry	Textile industry
Czechoslovakia	127	106	178[1]		173	126
France	113	112	113	99	–	98
Germany	182	169	196	241	194	121
Italy	144	140	168	198	243	107
Sweden	211	194	210	282	200	184
United Kingdom	153	95	170	188	148	119
Belgium	135	126	142	141	189	114
Europe without USSR	150	121	158	162	174	115

Note: [1] Metallurgy and Engineering
Sources: Calculated from *Statistická ročenka Protektorátu Čechy a Morava* (Statistical yearbook of the Protectorate of Bohemia and Moravia) (1941), p. 185; and *Industrial statistics, OEEC 1900–1955* (Paris, 1955).

(B) Index of Czechoslovak industrial production, 1924–37 (in %)

	1924	1929	1937
Industry as a whole	100.0	100.0	100.0
Mining	12.6	11.0	10.5
Electricity	1.5	2.0	2.9
Metallurgy and engineering	17.9	23.0	25.3
Chemical industry	4.7	5.0	6.4
Mining, electricity, metallurgy, engineering and chemical industries	36.7	41.0	45.1
Other branches of industry	63.3	59.0	54.9
Textile industry	23.9	21.0	21.5

Source: Teichova, A., 'Structural and institutional change in the Czechoslovak economy 1918–1938', *Papers in East European Economics*, 6, 1972.

Although high in comparison with South-east Europe, the overall level of industrialisation in Czechoslovakia was modest compared with North-west Europe: it was only in Bohemia and Moravia-Silesia that Czechoslovak industry reached a level of efficiency comparable with that of the advanced industrial nations. Seen in historical perspective, Bohemia and Moravia underwent a process of industrial change in the nineteenth century which is typical of the industrial revolutions which took place in West Europe: beginning with the textile industry and spreading to industries processing agricultural produce (sugar, beer-brewing, distilling), the process then extended to the producer-goods industries (agricultural and textile machinery, iron and coal). All phases of industrialisation in Czechoslovakia were accompanied by a constant flow of additional workers and domestic capital supplied by the relatively advanced agricultural sector. And it was on this historical basis that the extraordinarily rapid growth of industrial production in the Czech Lands was based. However, in terms of economic output for Czechoslovakia as a whole, this could compensate neither for the negative effect of the west–east gradient of industrial production nor the collapse in industrial production as a result of the economic crisis. This is shown by the low average annual rate of growth (1.5 per cent) of total industrial output in Czechoslovakia between 1913 and 1937. In principle, it was not possible to overcome the crisis of the 1930s due to inadequate modernisation and the failure to implement the necessary restructuring measures.

The west–east gradient of economic development was clearly reflected in Czechoslovak industry. In this respect, Slovakia was more badly affected than the Czech Lands by changes in its economic structure. Before the First World War, Slovakia produced approximately 20 per cent of the entire Hungarian production within the framework of the Habsburg monarchy. It also contained more than half of the paper and cellulose industry and more than a quarter of Transleithania's iron industry. The relatively retarded Slovak iron industry in particular was almost brought to a standstill by Czech competition and its share in total Czechoslovak iron production dropped from approximately 10 per cent in 1919 to 2.7 per cent in 1926. As a result of this unequal competitive situation, there came to be an emphasis on agricultural production and raw material extraction in Slovakia with the forestry, wool, magnesite, iron, ores, mineral oil industries acting primarily as suppliers to the Czech economy, thus increasing the dependence of Slovakia on the Czech Lands. Between 1927 and 1929, Slovakia provided the market with 13–17 per cent of Czech industrial products. Accordingly, industrialisation in Slovakia took place in relatively isolated areas, in many cases with specialised products which supplemented the advanced Czech industries (that is, cables, rubber products, wood distillation). According to official Czechoslovak statistics for 1926, only 9.1 per cent of all companies in Czechoslovakia with more than 18 employees were to be found in Slovakia. These companies had only 7.6 per cent of the population employed in industrial undertakings and accounted for only 7.5 per cent of the country's power consumption.

Whereas Slovak industry and banking were in the hands of German and Hungarian entrepreneurs before the First World War, Czech industrialists and bankers attained a decisive share of the Slovak economy between the two world wars. This resulted in the differences between Czechs and Slovaks in the economic sphere. Slovak entrepreneurs competed for more effective participation in their regional economy and for a greater share in the Czechoslovak domestic market. However, the structural changes in the interwar years emphasised the agricultural character of Slovakia in relation to Bohemia and Moravia which, in turn, increased the tendency towards underdevelopment of the whole domestic market in Czechoslovakia. Seen as part of the long-term process of development, it was disadvantageous that the west–east gradient of industrialisation was neither eliminated nor noticeably reduced up to 1938.

The structure of industry

The initial rapid rise in industrial production was accompanied by moves to introduce labour-saving devices in the production process, to reduce the costs of production and to improve profit margins which thus gave renewed impetus to the trend to rationalisation and concentration in Czechoslovak industry. Although this trend had not been insignificant in the Czech Lands since the turn of the century, the growth of larger enterprises and cartels spread to almost all branches of Czechoslovak industry during the interwar years. This process of concentration had differing effects on the individual branches of industry, ranging from an effective oligopolistic structure in iron and steel to widespread dispersion in the food-processing, textile and clothing industries.

Due to the lack of a long series of statistics, it is not possible to quantify continuous lines of development. However, the census of 1930 does provide a basis for a static overview. On census day, 27 May 1930, a total of 378,015 mining and industrial enterprises were counted. The overwhelming majority — 336,577 undertakings employing between one and five people — consisted of handicraft workshops or small specialist establishments, mainly in the food-processing, wood, clothing and leather industries. Almost a quarter (69,739) of these enterprises operated from private dwellings, within the framework of the putting-out system, but used only 0.1 per cent of all power consumed by industrial undertakings. The dwarf and small operations with up to five employees represented 89 per cent of all enterprises but used only 10.5 per cent of all power produced. On the other hand, the 41,438 units with six or more employees, that is, 11 per cent of all industrial enterprises, consumed 89.5 per cent of all power consumed by Czechoslovakia's industry.

Although self-employment and small enterprises continued to play a significant role, the overwhelming majority of Czechoslovak workers were employed in the medium-sized to large-scale undertakings. Despite the relatively widespread distribution of medium-sized enterprises, a tendency towards concentration is clearly visible from the opposing direction taken by the number of enterprises and the employment figures. Enterprises with more than 501 employees represented only 1.1 per cent of all undertakings but employed almost 30 per cent of all workers and accounted for half of the total industrial power consumption (see Table 3.10).

Similar trends can also be seen in the organisation and capital structure of industrial companies. In the period from 1919 to 1937, total share capital increased by a factor of four compared with only a doubling of the number of joint-stock companies. In comparison with the financial strength of private limited companies (*spol.s r.o.*), joint-stock companies (*uč.spol.*) display a much more concentrated structure. Whereas the total number of private limited companies in Czechoslovakia was a third more than the number of public companies, their total nominal

Table 3.10: Industrial enterprises according to number employed and horsepower used in Czechoslovakia, 27 May 1930

Enterprises according to number of persons employed	Enterprises		Workers employed		Motive power	
	No.	%	No.	%	In HP	%
6–20	28,612	69.0	262,326	15.6	189,030	7.3
21–50	7,020	17.0	223,358	13.3	196,963	7.5
51–100	2,905	7.0	202,617	12.2	247,351	9.5
101–250	1,833	4.4	281,144	16.8	357,951	13.7
251–500	622	1.5 } 2.6	213,667	12.7 } 42.1	314,650	12.0
501 and more	446	1.1 }	492,160	29.4 }	1,299,898	50.0
Total	41,438	100.0	1,675,272	100.0	2,605,843	100.0

Source: Based on *Československá statistika*, 117, 118, 119 (Prague, 1935).

share capital was only a tenth of the total nominal share capital of all joint-stock companies.

As part of the process of concentration, companies developed a pyramid corporate structure which created opportunities for wide-ranging connections within the Czechoslovak economy itself, as well as favourable conditions for further capital expansion in South-east Europe, via the subsidiary companies of Czechoslovak banks and industrial concerns. This formed a significant incentive for foreign investors and was further reinforced by the comparatively low cost of labour, the relatively stable political conditions of a bourgeois democratic system, as well as the strategic and geographical position of the ČSR.

Consequent upon the victory of the Entente powers in the First World War, changes took place in the capital structure of the Czechoslovak economy. The previously decisive spheres of influence held by Austria and Germany were weakened and, above all, Czech financial and industrial interests strengthened. In turn, these interests allied themselves with leading financial groups from Britain, France, Belgium and the United States. Through direct investments, approximately a quarter of the Czechoslovak economy came to be in the hands of foreign investors (British, French, Belgian, Dutch) during the interwar years. Table 3.11 shows the countries of origin of foreign capital investments in Czechoslovakia's industry and banking sector on

Table 3.11: Direct foreign long-term investments in Czechoslovak industry and banking, 31 December 1937

Origin of foreign investment	Total foreign investments, kč 3,191,904,000 — 100% (foreign investments amount to 27% of the total capital investments in Czechoslovak industry) %
Great Britain	30.8
France	21.4
Austria	13.1
Holland	8.8
Germany	7.2
Belgium	7.1
Switzerland	4.5
USA	3.5
Italy	2.2
Sweden	0.9
Hungary	0.5
Total	100.0
West European long-term investments	68.1

Source: A. Teichova, *An economic background to Munich: International business and Czechoslovakia* (Cambridge, 1974) (compiled from Table IV, p. 48).

the eve of the Second World War. The interest of foreign investors was principally in joint-stock companies and, at the end of 1937, foreign capital investments amounted to 27 per cent of total share capital in Czechoslovakia. Only 10 per cent of all public companies were directly involved with foreign capital; their total share capital represented 48 per cent of the total capital stock of all companies in industry, trade, transport and banking. This points to a significant degree of capital concentration and, simultaneously, is an indication that in the majority of cases foreign capital penetrated the financially strongest companies.

Branch structure of industry

The Czechoslovak metallurgy industry was the most highly concentrated industry not only within the framework of the national economy but also on an international plane. Fifty-three per cent of all joint-stock companies in the mining and metallurgy industry — which were closely interlinked — were recipients of direct foreign investment. However, this figure takes on a completely different dimension when it is considered that the basic nominal capital of these companies represented 98 per cent of the total. Accordingly, foreign investments alone amounted to 64 per cent of total nominal capital in this industry (see Table 3.12). The key position of the mining and metallurgy

Table 3.12: Foreign long-term investments in Czechoslovak industry as a percentage of the total share capital in the various branches of industry, 31 December 1937

Branches of industry	% of total share capital
Mineral oil and synthetic fats	97
Mining and metallurgy	64
Electrotechnical industry	52
Chemical industry	46
Engineering	40
Textiles	29
Building materials	22
Glass, porcelain, ceramics	18
Food industry	17
Paper industry	16
Commercial companies	9
Transport companies	5
Insurance societies	26
Banking	15
In industry as a whole	32

Source: As in Table 3.11, (Table III, p. 46).

industry in the Czechoslovak economy is evident from the results of the 1930 census which show that this industry employed 11 per cent of the working population and consumed 20 per cent of the power mechanically transmitted to working machines. The share of metallurgical products in total exports from Czechoslovakia rose from 12.5 per cent to 15 per cent between 1934 and 1937.

The extraordinary tendency in the Czechoslovak metallurgy industry towards concentration was based on the growth of the three largest concerns — The 'Big Three' — in which British and French capital played a decisive and German capital a not insignificant role. These companies dominated a well-organised and effective national cartel — the Prodejna sdružených československých železáren — which was probably the most comprehensive and tightest monopoly structure within the International Steel Cartel. From a 65 per cent share of steel production when the cartel was formed in 1921, the 'Big Three' came to hold 90 per cent after it had been in existence for 15 years. The cartel represented the Czechoslovak iron and steel industry in all international negotiations and the share of the export quotas in the International Steel Cartel was allocated exclusively to the 'Big Three'.

As one of the main branches of industry with relatively modern plant and equipment, the metallurgy industry formed the basis of a technically advanced mechanical and electrical engineering industry, as well as many other branches of industry in pre-Munich Czechoslovakia. According to calculations which primarily concern the immediate pre-war and post-war years, on average, the domestic mechanical engineering industry consumed half of the country's rolled steel production. A further 18 per cent was consumed by the building, transport, handicrafts and service industries, while approximately 32 per cent of all Czechoslovak rolled-steel production was exported. In common with developments in other industrially advanced countries, there was a trend to amalgamation between the supplier and consumer industries. As a rule, the metallurgy industry took on the leading role in this process of vertical concentration, either through buying up majority holdings in the foundries, cable, chain, nail, locomotive and bridge-construction factories, as well as in mechanical engineering and electrical engineering works, or through incorporation into cartels controlled by the metallurgy companies or through both methods.

The Czechoslovak mechanical engineering industry was relatively diversified. At the one end of the spectrum, there was a large number of medium-sized and small factories and workshops. At the other end of the scale, there was a high degree of concentration. As in other branches of industry, foreign capital also participated in the strongest and most highly concentrated companies of the mechanical engineering industry. The most important foreign investment in this sector was the decisive holding of the French iron and steel concern, Schneider Creusot,

41

in Czechoslovakia's leading mechanical engineering, electrical engineering and armaments concern, the Škoda Works. The Škoda Works not only held first place in the Czechoslovak mechanical engineering industry but their significance in East Central and South-east Europe can be compared with Vickers in Great Britain, Schneider in France and Krupp in Germany. The expansion of the Škoda Works into one concern, which basically controlled the whole of the mechanical engineering industry, was primarily pursued through the purchase of companies or majority holdings in companies at home and abroad between 1921 and 1938. The high point of these endeavours was reached in 1935 when, after a long and strenuous competitive struggle, an agreement was reached with the Škoda Works' biggest competitor in the domestic market, the Kolben-Daněk Company. This agreement covered all major Czechoslovak manufacturers and, in practice, rounded off the process of concentration in the mechanical engineering and armaments industry before the Second World War. Through the major holding of the Schneider Creusot concern in the Škoda Works, French influence penetrated not only the mechanical engineering industry in Czechoslovakia but also the whole of this sector throughout East Central and South-east Europe.

Like the mechanical engineering industry, the Czechoslovak chemical industry was dominated by one concern, the Spolek pro chemickou a hutní výrobu (Association for Chemical and Metallurgical Production), the largest chemical company in Central and South-east Europe after Germany's IG Farben-Industrie AG and which, through investments and patents, was closely linked to the Belgian Solvay Company. Their joint subsidiary companies were spread through all countries of Southeast Europe. Unrelenting competition between the world's mightiest chemical trusts led them to divide up their interests between them. In relation to production and sales, these divisions of interests were based on very complicated and, in many cases, obscure capital relationships and cartel agreements. In the case of Czechoslovakia, the chemical industry held an almost symbolic position in the economic structure of the country. Whereas the leading concerns were linked with Belgian, British and French capital, 60 per cent of all cartel agreements made by the Czechoslovak chemical industry with foreign partners were concluded with its greatest competitor, the German chemical industry.

The petroleum and vegetable-oil industry was closely connected with the chemical industry. All major manufacturers in this sector in Czechoslovakia were completely controlled by foreign capital which acquired no less than 97 per cent of the total nominal share capital of this industry. This exceptionally large proportion of foreign investments was due to the almost complete dependence of Czechoslovak production on imports of raw materials and semi-manufactured products for further processing. The most marked concentration arose in the production of goods from vegetable oils and fats when, in a series of fusions between 1919 and 1938, the biggest company, Schicht Brothers from Ústí nad Labem, was taken over step by step by the Anglo-Dutch trust of Lever Brothers. The Schicht Works and its Czechoslovak subsidiaries employed a fifth of all workers in the chemical, mineral oil and vegetable oil industries and accounted for a quarter of the total nominal share capital. They controlled the production as well as the market for soap and vegetable-fat products in Czechoslovakia and South-east Europe. In the course of the 1930s, this concern became the Central and South-east European arm of the multinational trust of Lever Brothers and Unilever.

Of all other branches of industry — the bulk of which belonged to the consumer-goods industry — only the shoe industry, in which foreign capital played no important role, exhibited a similar degree of concentration. In 1929, Czechoslovak shoe production in enterprises employing more than 18 people amounted to some 47.7 million pairs (including rubber shoes). In 1937, the company Baťa in Zlín manufactured approximately 47.8 million pairs of shoes representing six-sevenths of the entire Czechoslovak production.

As is to be expected from these figures, the Baťa Works also held a monopoly position among Czechoslovakia's shoe exporters. With the exception of 1930, between 1928 and 1938, Czechoslovakia held first place among the world's leading shoe exporters after overtaking Great Britain and the United States.

The process of concentration gradually came to encompass almost all other branches of industry in Czechoslovakia, for example, textiles, glass, porcelain, ceramics, paper, food processing, wood, leather, etc. However, the process of concentration in these historical and — due to the nature of the production methods — scattered industries developed in other ways. Basically, there are two lines of development in the Czechoslovak case which gave rise to changes in economic structure. One line of development led via the principal Czechoslovak banks which, commercially and financially, controlled a whole range of dependent companies producing a variety of different products. The other line of development moved in the direction of cartelisation through agreements between manufacturers and, later, through legislation. The Czechoslovak expert on cartels, Ervin Hexner, estimated that even in the initial phase of the economic crisis of 1929–33 almost 70 per cent of Czechoslovak industry was linked to cartels. All the economic forces which reinforced the existing trend towards industrial concentration were given additional impetus by the extraordinarily long duration of the economic crisis in Czechoslovakia.

Cartelisation

Consequent upon the crisis and the long-drawn-out depression, many companies were forced to close down completely or — through the intervention of the Czechoslovak cartels — to have their production concentrated in more efficient or financially more powerful enterprises.

Actions of this nature were most likely to take place in those industries where a high degree of concentration already existed, such as in almost all branches of producer-goods industry. There were also cartels in many branches of consumer-goods industry. However, the extent of cartelisation was considerably less than in the iron, steel and chemical industries, and there was always a number of outsiders; indeed, it was even possible to found a new company. During the world economic crisis of 1929–33, the Czechoslovak government provided legislative support for cartelisation in those branches of industry which were still relatively competitive. Compulsory cartelisation was enacted by the government at the request of the biggest manufacturers in any given branch of industry, that is, those with the largest production shares. Outsiders were no longer allowed to produce these goods and entry into the cartelised industry was impossible without special official permission.

Compulsory cartelisation began in those industries with close links to agriculture when, in 1932, distillery production was regulated and quotas introduced among the sugar refineries. In the following years, the timber industry, milling, glass-making, textiles, brewing and many products of the food-processing industry were officially cartelised.

In the sphere of agricultural production, the process of state-aided cartelisation was completed by 1934. The first in this series of cartels was the sugar cartel of 1927 which laid down the volume of domestic production, wholesale prices and contingents for beet growers. A number of legislative steps taken between 1931 and 1934 to cartelise many aspects of agricultural production — from grain production and animal husbandry to dairy products — led to the government founding the Czechoslovak Grain Company. This gave rise to the tightest agricultural monopoly ever to have existed in the ČSR, formed by the leading organisations of the biggest agricultural co-operatives and directed by the Centrokooperativ.

In Czechoslovakia, cartels were an integral part of the economic structure. They were officially approved and supported by the Cartel Act of 1933 which required the registration of all valid cartel agreements. In 1933, there was a total of 538 cartels recorded in the Cartel Register of the Czechoslovak State Statistical Office. By 30 September 1938 the number had risen to 1,152. Of these cartels, 212 were agreed between Czechoslovak and foreign industrial and commercial companies. The number of cartels alone can only give a superficial indication of their presence in the economic system and says very little about their complicated influence on the working of the economy. To make a realistic assessment of their role in economic life, an analysis of the content of the various cartel agreements is of decisive importance. However, there can hardly be any doubt about increased tendency towards concentration as a result of cartel agreements which existed together with and alongside monopolistic or oligopolistic industrial companies.

Every cartel agreement can be regarded as an expression of the balance of economic power between the partners to the agreement at the time of its conclusion. However, the common interests of cartel partners are invariably directed towards effectively controlling the market for their products; in the 1930s, the Czechoslovak economy was practically fully cartelised either as a result of the normal economic process of cartelisation or state intervention.

Czechoslovak cartels participated in the majority of international cartels existing at that time. Hence, to a great extent, the Czechoslovak economy was integrated in the cartel structure of the world's most important producers between the two world wars. International cartel agreements formed one-fifth of all registered cartels valid in Czechoslovakia between 1926 and 1938. The countries of origin of the foreign partners in the 212 valid agreements show a strikingly large number of German companies which by far exceeds the number of cartel partners from any other nation (see Table 3.13). The biggest number of cartel agreements made between Czechoslovak and German manufacturers was concluded in those branches of industry in which Western direct capital investment was strongest, that is, in the chemical, mechanical engineering and electrical industries, as well as the mining and metallurgical industry. The content of these cartel agreements shows that German producers obtained an agreed share in the former export markets of Czechoslovak manufacturers in South-east Europe and, whenever possible, a guaranteed share for their products in the domestic market of Czechoslovakia (if this was not possible, the cartel partners usually reached agreement on mutual market protection). The impact of these cartel agreements can be seen in the structural changes which took place in the pattern of Czechoslovakia's foreign trade in the 1930s. Whereas German direct capital investments in Czechoslovak industry were low in comparison with West European interests (see Table 3.11), the influence of German cartels in the Czechoslovak economy was incomparably greater than that of their Western competitors. On the other hand, the concentrated and cartelised economy of Czechoslovakia can by no means be described as being completely at the mercy of competing foreign financiers. The participation of national Czechoslovak cartels in the main international cartel agreements indicates that Czechoslovak industrial capacity was taken just as seriously as the country's economic and political significance for Central and South-east Europe during the interwar years.

BANKING

The structure of banking in Czechoslovakia between the two world wars was characterised by a large number of different types of bank. In principle, however, Czechoslovak banking can be divided into two main groups: the savings banks and the commercial banks with the latter group including joint-stock banks, limited companies and private banks (see Tables 3.14 and 3.15).

A major part of private savings was deposited with the numerous and widely dispersed small savings banks (credit co-operatives; citizens' trade and savings institutes; people's savings banks, etc.). As in the case of the co-operative movement, these small savings banks have their historical roots in the Czech national movement in Bohemia and Moravia during the second half of the nineteenth century. Above all, they represented economic rallying points for the Czech petty bourgeoisie. The structure of the savings banks is shown in Table 3.14. They totalled 7,414 in 1929 and 8,000 in 1935, compared with the total of 141 commercial banks in 1929 which dropped to 105 in 1935 (the structure of these banks is shown in Table 3.15).

A casual comparison of total deposits in savings accounts with other banks (see Tables 3.14 and 3.15) could lead to the erroneous conclusion that the savings banks were a significant financial power. In reality, because they were decentralised and distributed in small units and large numbers over the whole of Czechoslovakia, the savings banks were neither an effective leading force in Czechoslovak banking nor in the field of finance. However, they provided accumulated capital for the big banks which held the actual reins of financial and economic power.

In 1929, no more than 9 of the 23 Czech joint-stock banks ranked among the most influential in the country and, in reality, the decisive economic influence was only exercised by three banks: the Živnostenská Bank, the mightiest finance centre of the First Czechoslovak Republic, the Anglo-Czechoslovak and Prague Credit Bank and the Agrarian Bank. To a large degree, their leading position can be deduced from the accumulation and concentration of financial resources in these banks, as well as from the fact that the majority of other banks and numerous subsidiary companies were dependent on them to different extents and in different ways. Czech joint-stock banks had acquired extensive direct long-term holdings in industrial enterprises, transport firms and commercial companies and, at the same time, the biggest banks in Czechoslovakia headed major industrial concerns.

The development whereby joint-stock banks began to found and take shares in industrial enterprises and other companies had its roots in the Austro-Hungarian monarchy and, in accordance with the relationship between the Czech and Austrian

Table 3.13: Survey of cartel agreements of Czechoslovak industrial and commercial companies with foreign firms, 1926 to September 1938

Year of cartels' registration	Number of cartel agreements	Total number of cartel partners	ČSR	Germany	Austria	France	Poland	Great Britain	Belgium	Hungary	Italy	Holland
1926	7	76	21	13	9	7	3	6	3	3	2	1
1927	12	193	67	89	12	6	–	2	6	6	–	1
1928	7	47	22	17	7	–	–	–	–	–	1	–
1929	11	48	22	11	7	3	–	1	1	2	7	1
1930	23	222	63	61	9	33	9	5	8	5	3	1
1931	13	107	32	32	9	3	3	4	4	6	3	4
1932	11	111	46	20	9	2	15	3	–	8	2	1
1933	36	221	82	61	16	12	14	19	3	3	2	–
1934	25	142	39	19	8	15	9	16	14	6	3	8
1935	16	105	37	14	16	1	6	5	13	–	–	2
1936	21	162	119	19	5	1	7	1	–	4	7	–
1937	21	149	42	37	14	12	6	4	3	5	2	2
1938	9	72	18	20	2	–	12	2	9	1	–	4
Total	212	1,655	610	413	123	95	84	68	64	49	32	25

Nationality of cartel partners (spans ČSR through Holland columns)

Note: Total number of registered cartels up to 30 September 1938: 1,152. Source: Compiled from data in the Czechoslovak Cartel Register, SÚA-KR, Prague; cited in Teichova, *An economic background*, p. 56.

Nationality of cartel partners

Switzerland	USA	Sweden	Yugoslavia	Norway	Denmark	Spain	Canada	Romania	Finland	Luxembourg	Chile	USSR	Estonia
1	–	3	2	–	1	–	–	1	–	–	–	–	–
1	1	–	2	–	–	–	–	–	–	–	–	–	–
–	–	–	–	–	–	–	–	–	–	–	–	–	–
–	–	–	–	–	–	–	–	–	–	–	–	–	–
3	11	2	–	–	1	2	2	–	–	–	–	–	–
1	–	1	–	2	2	–	–	–	1	–	–	–	–
1	–	–	2	1	–	–	–	–	–	–	–	–	–
5	–	–	2	–	–	2	–	2	–	–	–	–	–
1	1	–	1	1	–	–	–	–	–	1	1	–	–
1	–	2	1	1	–	–	–	1	1	–	–	1	–
2	–	2	–	–	–	2	–	–	–	–	–	–	–
7	2	3	–	1	1	2	–	–	–	–	–	–	1
1	–	–	–	1	–	–	–	–	–	–	–	–	–
24	15	13	10	7	5	5	4	3	2	1	1	1	1

Table 3.14: Structure of people's savings banks in Czechoslovakia (in kč millions)

	Saving banks in ČSR	District agricultural saving banks	Citizens' and tradesmen's banks
Number of Institutions	356	174	1,909
			Liabilities
Shares	–	39.3	252.1
Reserves and other funds	1,426.6	216.9	767.3
Deposits on savings books	18,810.3	4,029.6	12,148.1
Creditors	3,004.7	357.8	1,585.9
Other liabilities	121.5	24.7	104.6
Profits	111.0	8.2	58.9
			Assets
Cash	116.2	30.9	117.9
Immediate claims	3,368.0	666.2	1,986.9
Bills	5,889.6	316.8	1,070.5
Loans	12,688.3	3,452.3	10,802.4
Immovable assets	493.8	96.8	660.5
Other assets	910.0	113.5	268.4
Losses	8.2	–	10.3
Total assets/ liabilities	23,474.1	4,676.5	14,916.9

Note: [1] Saving institutions.
Source: M. Ubiria-VI. Kadlec-J. Matas, *Peněžni a úvěrová soustava Československa za kapitalismu* (Money and credit in Czechoslovakia during capitalism) (Prague, 1958), p. 341.

Kampeličky[1]	Credit co-operatives in Slovakia	Total for 1935	Total for 1929
4,371	1,190	8,000	7,414
Liabilities			
11.9	55.0	358.3	290.0
203.2	44.0	2,658.0	1,660.2
4,924.5	938.7	40,851,2	36,662.0
238.5	368.2	5,551.1	3,581.3
19.7	15.7	286.2	344.1
17.2	4.9	204.2	271.5
Assets			
60.8	23.2	349.0	391.9
1,180.2	245.1	7,446.4	6,703.2
180.6	16.8	7,474.3	5,988.0
3,743.8	1,092.3	31,779.1	27,849.0
82.9	21.4	1,355.4	701.3
166.2	28.4	1,484.5	1,125.9
0.5	1.3	20.3	10.7
5,415.0	1,426.5	49.909.0	42,770.0

Table 3.15: Structure of Czechoslovak banks (in kč millions)

	Joint-stock banks in Czech Lands	Banks without joint-stock capital
Number of banks	23	9
		Liabilities
Joint-stock capital or capital stock	1,266.7	56.0
Reserves and other funds	1,125.5	356.1
Bonds	487.1	5,974.7
Deposits	8,814.6	1,879.5
Creditors	12,195.7	4,100.7
Other liabilities	502.2	134.6
Profits	76.8	11.4
Total liabilities and assets	24,468.6	12,513.0
		Assets
Cash and immediate claims	3,202.0	661.8
Bills	2,987.9	2,348.7
Investments	801.8	–
Debtors	15,835.9	3,356.3
Loans emissions	517.0	5,942.1
Immovable assets	624.5	79.0
Other Assets	377.5	125.1
Losses	122.0	–

Source: As for Table 3.14, p. 340.

Joint-stock banks in Slovakia	Limited companies, banking houses, bankers	Total for 1935	Total for 1929
57	16	105	141
	Liabilities		
250.4	22.4	1,595.7	2,322.4
152.3	5.3	1,539.2	2,078.1
–	–	6,461.8	4,563.3
2,346.5	–	13,040.4	13,154.4
760.8	184.3	17,241.5	21,962.7
23.3	2.6	662.7	1,147.1
15.1	1.3	104.6	318.8
3,548.4	215.9	40,745.9	45,546.8
	Assets		
415.3	22.9	4,302.0	3,402.2
351.2	37.6	5,725.9	4,813.3
76.1	0.4	873.3	1,172.5
2,428.3	131.6	21,756.5	30,415.2
–	–	6,459.2	4,538.5
219.7	6.2	929.4	682.6
46.5	1.7	550.8	521.7
11.3	15.5	148.8	0.8

financial communities existing at that time, the Viennese banks came to hold a central position in the biggest banking and industrial concerns. The sole exception was the Živnostenská Bank which, through capital investments in predominantly domestic companies, came to head a purely Czech industrial concern. With the collapse of the Habsburg monarchy and the foundation of the First Czechoslovak Republic, Czech bankers immediately sought to sever their financial and capital links with Vienna and to gain possession of as many as possible of the financial and industrial holdings of the great Viennese banks within the borders of the new state. These efforts were introduced with the Currency Separation Law of 1919 (see p. 67) and facilitated by the nostrification and nationalisation laws which, although they played a role throughout the existence of the First Republic, were applied most intensively between 1919 and 1921. In this way, the big joint-stock banks were able to spin a web of financial, credit and capital relations with varying degrees of dependence across almost all branches of Czechoslovak industry.

As a result of post-war developments and incorporation into the new economic spheres of influence, fundamental changes also took place in the structure of international banking. The major Czechoslovak joint-stock banks reflect quite accurately the relative changes in political influence which took place among the main groups in the world of international finance. The position previously held by Austrian, German and Hungarian banks in the Czech and Slovak economic sphere was taken over by Czech banks. At the same time, however, many holdings were taken over by banks and financial groups from the Entente powers. The seats on the boards of directors of Czechoslovak banks relinquished by Austrians, Germans and Hungarians were filled by representatives of Czech, British, French, American, Belgian, Dutch and Italian banks.

On the one hand, Western capital assisted Czechoslovak bankers and industrialists to consolidate their position against their former competitors. On the other hand, leading personalities in Czechoslovakia's economic sector tried to achieve at least partial independence from the influence of foreign capital. The question is how successful they were in this. It seems almost certain that domestic financial groups succeeded in enlarging the scope of their holdings in Czechoslovak banks at the expense of foreign capital investors during the economic crisis when the large banks amalgamated with considerable support and subsidies from the state. This led to even greater concentration in the banking sector. While this process was taking place, the Czechoslovak banks took over further Austrian investments in the domestic economy, in particular from the Österreichische Boden-Kredit-Anstalt and the Österreichische Credit-Anstalt für Handel und Gewerbe which went bankrupt in 1930–31 taking the whole of the Austrian economy with them. In many cases, Czechoslovak banks invested themselves in Central and South-east Europe. In the majority of cases, however, they did so in conjunction with their foreign partners. Accordingly, although Czechoslovak banks were sometimes independent capital investors, they were more often participants in Western financial groups or mediators for such groups operating through Prague banks.

One of the main characteristics of the Czechoslovak banking system between the two world wars was the role of the most powerful joint-stock banks as the heads of important industrial concerns which firmly linked the whole of Czechoslovakia's industry with its banks.

FOREIGN TRADE

In comparison with the advanced Western industrial nations, which, as a rule, were able to convert their negative trade balances into positive figures thanks to income from invisible earnings, Czechoslovakia's capital balance was negative and, in order to cover the foreign currency requirements, a positive balance of trade was essential. As can be seen from the balance of payments statistics of pre-Munich Czechoslovakia, there was a positive balance of trade for the whole interwar period with the exception of 1932 (see Table 3.16). Under the conditions of buoyant economic growth between 1927 and 1929, almost one-third of the national income derived from the export sector.

Until 1928, developments in the Czechoslovak export sector progressed relatively better than in the rest of Europe. On the basis of market prices, exports rose by 45.8 per cent between 1913 and 1928 compared with the European average of 41.4 per cent. Czechoslovakia's role in world trade was relatively small and only slightly more significant in European terms. In 1927, the Czechoslovak share of world exports amounted to 1.93 per

Table 3.16: Excerpts from Czechoslovak balances of payments, 1924–37 (in kč millions)

Year	Merchandise	Services	Long- and short-term capital	Interest and dividends	Total of balance of payments
1924	+1,200	+600		−670	+1,130
1925	+1,212	+ 95	− 373	−739	+ 517
1926	+2,575	+100	−1,304	−814	+1,925
1927	+2,172	+591	−2,316	−697	+1,972
1928	+2,023	+612	−1,903	−571	+1,905
1929	+ 520	+722	− 844	−361	+ 757
1930	+1,779	+511	− 316	−572	+1,415
1931	+1,373	− 1	+ 852	−356	+ 887
1932	− 144	+158	+ 294	−281	− 326
1933	+ 21	+262	+ 328	−330	− 45
1934	+ 898	+269	− 183	−331	+ 327
1935	+ 680	− 24	− 236	−478	+ 170
1936	+ 99	−112	− 355	−546	− 462
1937	+ 992	− 78	− 595	−514	+ 337

Source: League of Nations, Balances of Payments, relevant years.

cent and of European exports to 4.2 per cent. However, Czechoslovakia held a special position among the countries of Central and South-east Europe. Historically, the country's industrial structure in the Danube basin had developed in accordance with the needs of the primarily agricultural region of South-east Europe for industrial goods. Even at the end of 1921, approximately half of Czechoslovakia's exports went to the Successor States. Although the importance of this region began to fall in the following years, the characteristic features, which were specific to the structure of the Czechoslovak economy and foreign trade, remained more or less intact until the economic crisis. On the one hand, Czechoslovakia appears in the foreign trade statistics as a typical industrial nation. On the other hand, however, the country's considerable exports of industrial goods were not — as in the other advanced countries of the world — balanced by extensive imports of agricultural products. The position of the agricultural sector in the national economy was so great that a significant and, with time, increasing part of home demand could be met from domestic sources. At the same time, Czechoslovakia exported the bulk of its production of barley, malt, hops and sugar. On the import side, Czechoslovakia mostly purchased raw materials overseas while advanced machinery, equipment, vehicles and chemical products from Western countries were of major importance for the country's industrial production, that is, Czechoslovakia's exports had a significant import content.

Thus, the structure of the Czechoslovak economy and foreign trade provided no solid basis for trade relations with the agricultural economies of Central and South-east Europe, which had been the traditional consumers of Czechoslovak industrial production.

Reciprocal trade with the Successor States between the two wars was further impeded by Czechoslovakia's tariff policy. In 1925, the Czechoslovak Government introduced a sliding scale of tariffs for grain, mill products and lard after a clash of economic interests between representatives of industry and agriculture from which the latter emerged victorious. Following further economic and political triumphs by the agrarian interests, in 1926, this was replaced by a stable system of protective tariffs for agricultural products, in which a minimum — below which the duty could not sink — was set for every individual product. Consequently, imports of agricultural products to Czechoslovakia from the countries of South-east Europe began to drop. Simultaneously, the situation of the Czechoslovak export economy became more complicated due to the gradual industrialisation of the Successor States which, as in Czechoslovakia, was promoted by imports of capital from the West European countries and accompanied by a tendency towards economic nationalism. In their search for outlets for their agricultural products, the Successor States, in particular the Balkan countries, began to look to Germany as a potential trading partner; especially after 1926 when Germany's industry rapidly expanded and once again became a serious competitor in the markets of Central and South-east Europe.

The impact of the economic crisis on foreign trade and its particularly negative impact on Czechoslovak exports (see Table 3.17) underlined the existing tendencies in the Czechoslovak economy and exposed the inherent structural contradictions. The structural changes in exports from Czechoslovakia, as illustrated in the table, show a great drop (17.5 per cent) in the products of consumer goods and food-processing industries, in particular, textiles, clothing, sugar, malt and oats. On the other hand, the percentage share of exports from the iron, steel and

Table 3.17: Percentage share of various industries in total Czechoslovak exports, 1929 and 1937

Industries	1929		1937	
Products of consumer goods		60.7		43.2
Share of: Textile and clothing industry	34.5		21.5	
Glass and ceramic industry	9.2		8.8	
Leather and leather products	6.9		5.3	
Sugar, malt and oats	10.1		7.6	
Products of producer goods industries		15.4		25.2
Share of: Iron, other metals	11.6		18.9	
Machines, instruments, tools, cars	3.8		6.3	
Products of other industries		23.9		31.6
Total		100.0		100.0

Source: Computed from *Zahraniční obchod Republiky československé* (Foreign trade of the Czechoslovak Republic), I (1929 and 1937).

metal-working industries rose by almost 10 per cent. At the same time, as the impact of the existing tendencies was being felt in full, changes also took place in the territorial distribution of Czechoslovak foreign trade. The most important change was the constant increase in the volume of foreign trade in non-European markets (see Table 3.18). Particularly indicative was the relative drop in the share of Germany and the Successor States in Czechoslovak foreign trade between 1924 and 1937: Germany's share fell from 32.9 per cent to 16.4 per cent and that of the Successor States from 32.21 per cent to 19.25 per cent of total Czechoslovak foreign trade (compare Table 3.19). The reason for the reduced level of trade with South-east Europe has already been mentioned. Polemical discussions about the causes and effects of these structural changes still continue. However, few publications deal directly with the fact that, although trade between the Danube countries dropped relatively, there was little change in absolute terms. In Czechoslovak–German relations, despite its declining share in Czechoslovak foreign trade, Germany remained the most important country in the statistics of Czechoslovak foreign trade: the Czechoslovak balance of trade with Germany was negative until 1937, whereby Germany accounted for a fifth of all Czechoslovak trade from 1920 to 1938. The drop in trade with Germany during the 1930s was mostly a direct consequence of the German policy of autarky. In addition, certain groups of influential Czechoslovak exporters consciously endeavoured to reduce their trade contacts with Germany due, on the one hand, to the increasing aggressiveness of German foreign trade policy and the fact that there was no official trade treaty between the two states. On the other hand, these groups hoped to redirect Czechoslovak foreign trade towards the Western powers, in accordance with the political orientation of their government. These efforts ran into insurmountable difficulties due to the

Table 3.18: Territorial distribution of Czechoslovak foreign trade by continents, 1924–37 (in %)

Continent	1924		1929		1937	
	Import	Export	Import	Export	Import	Export
Europe	91.9	90.5	85.0	84.2	69.1	74.1
Germany[1]	35.2	19.5	25.0	19.4	15.5	13.7
Successor States[2]	23.7	40.3	23.2	35.1	16.7	29.9
Britain and France	6.2	11.0	7.9	8.5	11.6	12.5
Asia	1.4	2.9	4.0	3.9	9.1	7.0
Africa	0.3	1.0	1.9	1.8	4.9	3.9
America	6.4	5.5	8.5	9.9	15.3	14.3
USA	5.6	4.2	5.5	7.2	8.7	9.3
Australia and Oceania	0.0	0.1	0.6	0.2	1.6	0.7

Note: [1] Without ports; [2] Austria, Hungary, Romania, Yugoslavia, Poland.
Source: *Československá statistika* 67 (1931) and 164 (1938).

Table 3.19: Percentage share of Germany and the Successor States in Czechoslovak foreign trade, 1924–37

Country	1924	1929	1932	1934	1935	1936	1937
Germany and harbours	32.19	30.15	27.78	24.27	19.39	19.12	16.14
Austria	14.52	11.46	9.54	8.01	7.51	6.73	5.81
Hungary	6.14	5.62	2.08	2.06	1.92	1.89	1.69
Poland	3.90	5.41	3.57	2.72	3.59	2.42	2.20
Yugoslavia	3.80	3.70	5.10	3.35	4.81	4.89	4.38
Romania	3.85	3.07	4.09	3.34	4.54	4.66	5.17
Total	32.21	29.26	24.38	19.48	22.37	20.59	19.25

Source: *Zahraniční obchod Republiky československé*; *Čs. statistika*, II (Prague, 1938), p. 35.

Table 3.20: Comparative share of Czechoslovakia and Germany in the total imports of Central and South–east European states, 1928 and 1935 (in %)

Country	Share of Czechoslovakia		Share of Germany	
	1928	1935	1928	1935
Austria	18.4	12.8	19.9	16.6
Hungary	22.4	5.1	19.5	22.9
Yugoslavia	18.0	14.5	13.7	16.9
Romania	14.5	13.4	23.6	23.7
Bulgaria	10.5	8.0	20.9	54.1
Turkey	6.2	4.3	14.5	40.0

Source: A. Teichova, 'Über das Eindringen des deutschen Finanzkapitals in das Wirtschaftsleben der Tschechoslowakei vor dem Münchener Diktat', *Zeitschrift für Geschichtswissenschaft*, V/6 (1957).

protectionist policies of Czechoslovakia's allies, especially France and Great Britain.

In Czechoslovakia's traditional markets in South-east Europe, German competition increased noticeably after 1928 (see Table 3.20). This led to the Czechoslovak and German shares in the imports of the South-east European countries moving in opposite directions. Table 3.21 shows their relative shares in the imports and exports of the Little Entente states.

At all events, the German share of South-east European foreign trade rose while the Czechoslovak share fell. The exception to the rule in this case is Romania, the exports of which to Czechoslovakia increased slightly, whereas its exports to Germany dropped markedly. However, at the same time Romanian imports from Germany rose, while there was a drop in imports from Czechoslovakia (see Table 3.21). In order to replace their losses in Europe, Czechoslovak exporters increasingly turned their attention to markets in Asia, Africa and America (see Table 3.18).

This structural change in foreign trade was not without impact on Czechoslovakia's industry, above all in regard to the scope of production in the consumer goods industry which was hit particularly severely by the sinking exports.

Industrial production stagnated in those branches of industry which were mainly dependent on exports and, consequent on the permanent drop in demand for their products in the world markets, they were unable to attain their previous levels of production. Persistent depression reigned in the Czechoslovak consumer goods industry — especially in the textile, glass and porcelain sectors — with high unemployment and falling incomes. Because industrial capacity was not evenly distributed throughout the country, these industries were chiefly to be found in the western and north-western border regions of Czechoslovakia where the bulk of the German-speaking population had their homes. Due to the high level of unemployment and lower incomes, this segment of the population was more

Table 3.21: Comparative share of Germany and Czechoslovakia in the total imports and exports of the states of the Little Entente, 1929, 1932 and 1937 (in %)

Yugoslavia

Date	Import from		Export to	
	Germany	Czecho-slovakia	Germany	Czecho-slovakia
1929	30.0	17.5	24.1	5.4
1932	31.1	15.6	33.4	13.3
1937	42.7	11.1	35.2	7.9

Romania

Date	Import from		Export to	
	Germany	Czecho-slovakia	Germany	Czecho-slovakia
1929	36.6	13.6	37.0	6.2
1932	28.8	12.2	18.7	7.0
1937	38.0	10.1	26.9	8.4

Source: Marko Weirich, *Staré a nové Československo* (Old and new Czechoslovakia), (Prague, 1938–9).

badly hit than the average. The unfavourable economic consequences and the social privation which existed in these regions during the 1930s provided a fruitful basis for German nationalism and fascism under the leadership of Henlein's Sudeten German Party which was supported by National Socialist Germany materially and ideologically.

In comparison with 1929, the Czechoslovak economy exhibits a much more pronounced autarkic character in 1937. The level of foreign trade remained below that of 1929, whereas industrial production had almost regained the level of 1929. The result was a worsening of the Czechoslovak position in the world economy at a time of great military menace and contributed to the weakening of the country's political situation.

With regard to capital movements, Czechoslovakia represented the exception to the Central and South-east European rule. The country's industrial development, its economic structure and the process of industrial concentration had greater similarities to Germany and the other Western industrial nations than the neighbouring countries of South-east Europe. In common with the other industrial nations, Czechoslovakia was both an importer and exporter of capital with its capital exports traditionally being directed to the South-east. Under special conditions, Czechoslovakia also participated in the capital exports of other countries, in particular those of French and British industrial concerns, and, during the interwar years, Czechoslovakia formed an important link in the network of economic relationships between West, Central and South-east Europe.

TRANSPORT AND COMMUNICATIONS

For an inland state which was dependent on foreign trade to a large extent, the distance from sea ports such as Triest (832 kilometres from Prague), Stettin (450 kilometres from Prague) and Hamburg (780 kilometres from Prague) was a disadvantage that was mitigated by the internationalisation of the rivers (Danube, Oder, Elbe) and by the allocation of freely accessible docking spaces. Approximately 10 per cent of all exports and 10 per cent of total imports were conveyed by means of water transport. Furthermore, the geographical position of Czechoslovakia as a commercial transit area proved to be beneficial. To a certain extent, the extraordinary length of the country (930 kilometres) and its taper from west to east (from 280 kilometres to 40 kilometres) placed the western districts at an advantage because, in the transport network inherited from the monarchy, the major European trade routes linked Bohemia and Moravia with the south, north and west, while Slovakia and the Carpatho-Ukraine only had economically worthwhile connections to the south.

Particularly at the beginning of the 1920s, the connections between the Czech Lands and Slovakia were completely inadequate. In order to achieve a relatively coherent transport system, there was a direct relationship between the way borders were drawn and the railway connections of the new state. For example, on the Polish–Czechoslovak border, Těšín was divided in such a way that the only railway link between the Czech Lands and Slovakia existing at that time was awarded to Czechoslovakia. Among other factors, the need for an east–west railway connection influenced the way the border was drawn between Slovakia and Hungary, as a result of which some 500,000 Hungarians became citizens of the new Czechoslovak state.

In the transport sector, the railway was the most important means of transport both for people and goods throughout the First Republic. In 1920, the Czechoslovak railway system was the eighth biggest in Europe. However, in comparison to other countries, railway construction stagnated so that, by 1929, it had dropped to fifteenth place. Although the railway network survived the war unscathed, it had deteriorated to such an extent that, by 1922, only around 62 per cent of the locomotives and 88 per cent of the goods wagons could be made serviceable. In accordance with the programme of 1924, the railways were almost completely nationalised and improved but not 100 per cent standardised. All parts of the country were linked from east to west by two transverse railway lines. Altogether, only 350 kilometres of new lines were laid. However, many branch lines were upgraded into double-track main lines. Trade and industry profited from standardisation and price reductions, while the increasing losses of the railway network were covered by the Czechoslovak treasury.

With 500 kilometres per 1,000 square kilometres, the Czechoslovak road network came after that of Germany. On the other hand, the route length per 1,000 square kilometres in England and France was more than double as much, whereas the South-east European countries fell below the Czechoslovak standard. In the course of the interwar years, the quality of Czechoslovakia's roads was improved through asphalting or concreting. However, these improvements took place mainly on national or municipal roads which, in 1936, covered some 15,300 kilometres of the total length of 70,200 kilometres. Accordingly, Czechoslovakia remained way behind Germany and France in terms of motor-vehicle traffic despite the fact that it was a not insignificant automobile manufacturing state. Step by step, buses and trucks displaced horse transportation and motorised vehicles began to compete with the railways. In air transport, Czechoslovakia made only slow progress after 1923 and this mode of transportation remained insignificant until after the Second World War.

The earliest and most important instrument of long-distance communication was the telegraphic network. Its development proceeded alongside that of the railway and the system was fully on a par with those of Western Europe. Parallel with the expansion of the postal system, the number of telephone connections increased to 200,000 by 1937. However, the network only covered 42 per cent of the communities.

After 1926, the radio audience increased considerably and reached over 1 million by 1937. In Czechoslovakia, the communications system formed a component part of the government-controlled infrastructure.

In Central and South-east Europe, Czechoslovakia had the most advanced transportation and communications networks. As a result of the dismemberment of the Czechoslovak state in 1938 and 1939, they ceased to exist as independent entities with the individual parts being placed at the disposal of those states participating in the territorial spoils, above all Germany and Hungary.

4

The State

THE MAIN DIRECTIONS OF STATE ACTIVITY IN THE ECONOMY AND SOCIETY

Political stabilisation

The decisive factor governing the basic activities of the state in the economy and society was the development of Czechoslovakia as a bourgeois democratic republic based on the continuation of a capitalist, free-market economy. The first law of the new Czechoslovak state passed by the Czechoslovak National Committee on 28 October 1918 decreed that all existing 'Land' and 'Imperial' laws should continue in force. The aim of this measure was to ensure the smoothest possible transition to a parliamentary republic.

All the Successor States were threatened by revolution, civil war, uprisings and strikes with their demands for the redistribution of large estates and the socialisation of big enterprises and banks followed by a dismantling of the capitalist economic system. Although Czechoslovakia was no exception to this, with the strike movement reaching its peak in December 1920, the revolutionary movement was affected by the pronounced national sentiments of the population and the desire of the majority of them for autonomous statehood. Confidence in the future of the new state was reflected in the success of the 'National Liberation Loan'. Issued on 5 November 1918, the loan was immediately fully subscribed with 1 milliard crowns. The enthusiastic response accorded to the Liberation Loan was in complete contrast to that given the Austro-Hungarian loans between 1914 and 1918 which were largely boycotted in the Czech Lands. Placing further public loans also presented no problems, a fact which not only helped the government cover part of the budget deficit but also sucked in a part of the excess money in circulation. Even the Czechoslovak taxpayers reacted positively to the creation of an independent state during the first few years. Revenues were constantly higher than expected, despite the fact that the pre-war system of taxation had been retained and there was a steep increase in the rate of indirect taxation. This positive attitude to independence made it possible for the Czechoslovak government to implement its social and economic policies, although, at the beginning, major concessions — such as the land reform (see pp. 27–9), the introduction of the eight-hour day and extensive social reforms — had to be made, in order to guarantee economic and political control along the lines of the Western democracies.

The separation from Austria-Hungary

The outlines of an independent economic and political programme were drafted by the 'Men of 28 October' in the Czechoslovak National Committee before the disintegration of the Danube monarchy. However, due to the closely knit network of financial and capital relationships in the former Austro-Hungarian economy, it was impossible to realise these plans immediately in the newly formed republic. Having consolidated their government under the Presidency of Tomáš Garrigue Masaryk, Czechoslovakia's statesmen and leading industrialists were well aware of the potential economic might of the republic in comparison with other parts of the Habsburg monarchy. They did not want to be identified with the losers of the war and endeavoured to distance their state from the Central Powers and their post-war burden. Due to the contribution made by the Czechs and the Slovaks to the war effort of the Entente powers, they held out hopes of being given a share of the reparations. However, they were to be disappointed in this: although the Czechoslovak Republic did not have to pay any war debts, it was required to pay a share of the pre-war Austro-Hungarian debts and a 'Liberation Contribution'. In principle, the measures taken by the young state were aimed at releasing the ties which bound it to Vienna, the former financial centre of the Empire, and Budapest, as well as the creation of a distinctly separate Czechoslovak economy.

The immediate objective of the Czechoslovak government was to prevent Czechoslovakia being caught up in the whirlwind of the Austro-Hungarian inflation. On 2 November 1918, all branches of the Austro-Hungarian Bank on Czechoslovak territory were banned from redeeming war loans and, on 14 November, they were prohibited from making any payments to banks, with the exception of funds for paying wages and salaries. In addition, the right to pay taxes with war obligations was abolished. Parallel with these measures to limit the supply of money, the government severed all connections with the former central bank of the monarchy. Soon thereafter, the founding of the Czechoslovak Giro and Post Office Savings Bank and the Prague Stock Exchange (November–December 1918) contributed further to the establishment of independent control by the state over the Czechoslovak currency.

Stabilisation and nationalisation policy

Between February and April 1919 the Czechoslovak government took decisive steps to break the last links between the Czechoslovak and Austro-Hungarian economies through currency separation and reform. In accordance with the plan prepared by the Czechoslovak Minister of Finance, Dr Alois Rašín — the only successful, independent stabilisation policy among the Successor States — the Currency Separation Law came into force on 25 February 1919. Fifty per cent of all privately held bank notes were withdrawn; bank and savings accounts were blocked and converted into a 1 per cent compulsory loan. This went hand in hand with a property census, as a preparatory move prior to levying a property tax. In this case, however, patriotic enthusiasm alone proved to be insufficient. Delays, appeals and avoidance meant that the state was only able to gather in half of the expected 12 milliard Czechoslovak crowns. Payments of tax arrears, the property tax or expenditures arising from special permission could be paid from blocked accounts. As a result of these measures, although the hoped for 50 per cent could not be achieved, the money supply in Czechoslovakia did drop by 25 per cent. On 6 March 1919, the administration of the currency and coin monopoly was transferred from the Austro-Hungarian Bank in Vienna to the Banking Office of the Czechoslovak Ministry of Finance (Bankovní úřad ministerstva financí — BÚMF), the forerunner of the Czechoslovak National Bank (founded in 1926). A further currency law of 10 April 1919 introduced the Czechoslovak crown (kč) as the national currency and legal tender of the new republic. The currency reform had a stabilising effect, dampened the inflationary tendencies and, through the breakage of the economic dominance of Vienna and Budapest, created a framework for an independent Czechoslovak economy.

The land reform constituted an integral part of the Czechoslovak economic and social policy. Between April 1919 and April 1920 the Czechoslovak Parliament approved the main legislation and commissioned the Land Office with the introduction, administration and implementation of the land reform laws. As mentioned above (see p. 27), the land reform was the product of the political situation existing from 1917 to 1919. In Czechoslovakia, it provided support for Czech-nationalist elements and helped increase the efficiency of capitalist agricultural production.

The Czechoslovak government implemented its programme of nationalisation in industry and banking in this spirit. The programme aimed to reinforce domestic industry and replace socialisation with nationalisation. In other words, there was no intention of nationalising large private concerns and banks but rather, by means of a legal process known as nostrification, foreign, formerly enemy property was to be transferred into Czechoslovak hands. The Nostrification Law, which came into force at the end of 1919, forced joint-stock companies to transfer their head offices, in the most cases from Vienna, to the territory of the new state where they had their factories and industrial plant. Together with the currency reform and the banking laws of 1919, this law separated the major Viennese banks and concerns from their subsidiary companies in Czechoslovakia and created favourable conditions for Czech banks, above all the Živnostenská Bank, to acquire direct influence in these companies. A further law concerning joint-stock companies required that at least half of the members of the boards of directors be Czechoslovak citizens. In addition, the general director had not only to be a Czechoslovak citizen but also had to have his permanent place of residence in the First Republic. Czechoslovakia's economic policy in the field of capital transfers was also assisted by the Versailles Peace Treaty, according to paragraph 297 of which, as an Associated State, the Czechoslovak government was empowered to seize German investments in railways, foundries, iron and steel works and spa resorts. This process was completed with the Maximal Liquidation Programme of 1924.

At the same time, the Czechoslovak government — in correspondence with the orientation of its foreign policy towards the Entente powers and with the active support of the country's bankers and industrialists — sought to consolidate the political and economic situation with the aid of Entente investments and thus reduce German and Austrian influence in banking and industry. In the interests of the credit-worthiness of the state, the Czechoslovak government considered it essential to stabilise the currency on a long-term basis using national resources as far as possible. Objective conditions contributed to the attainment of this goal: the new state soon succeeded in achieving political stability; the balance of trade was positive after 1920; and, as inflationary prices started to recede in the post-war crisis of 1921, the government was able to pursue a deflationary policy. However, the Czechoslovak crown was relatively over-valued in 1922 and the republic's exports lost their competitive edge in the international market. This had a temporarily negative impact on the volume of production and the employment level. Only outside factors alleviated the harshness of the deflationary policy on the Czechoslovak economy. These factors consisted of a combination of events which occurred roughly in parallel, such as the success of the first tranche of the Czechoslovak Loan in Britain in 1922, the flight from the mark in 1923 which boosted the value of the crown, and the French occupation of the Ruhr which restricted Germany's exports, increased its import requirements and thus had an invigorating effect on Czechoslovakia's export industries. Between 1924 and 1926, Czechoslovakia joined those countries with stable currencies on the gold standard. As a result of the National Bank's regulative policy and its satisfactory gold and foreign currency reserves, Czechoslovakia ranked among the financially sound and reliable capitalist countries of the inter-war period. Without doubt, its monetary system was the most efficient in Central and Southeast Europe.

ECONOMIC POLICY

Fiscal policy

Apart from state monopolies such as tobacco, saccharin and explosives, direct participations by the state in industrial enterprises were insignificant. The investment policy of the Czechoslovak government gave priority to private industry. As a result of the extremely high public expenditures — for the formation of a modern army, for the reorganisation of the state machinery, for social services, as well as for the provision of public services — a healthy climate for private investment was created in the early 1920s. Certain amounts of these official expenditures were borne by international aid credits and foreign loans. However, the bulk of the initial household deficit was covered by state loans which were taken up by domestic banks and the general public. From 1924 on, the government reduced its requirement for domestic loans, thus releasing further funds for investment in the private sector.

In principle, despite the fact that Czechoslovak fiscal policy was in line with the objectives of a market economy, it was not carried out in accordance with any official economic theory. Born out of the war, the decision-makers in Czechoslovakia were less influenced by the general aims of the West European governments to return to the 'normality of pre-war days' than by pragmatic considerations. In common with other states, the Czechoslovak Republic strove to achieve a balanced budget (which, nevertheless, remained in deficit until 1926). With the outbreak of the economic crisis, it did not hold stubbornly on to a balanced-budget policy (see Table 4.1). Like other states, Czechoslovakia pursued a liberal economic policy. However, it is seldom appreciated how much more firmly the Czechoslovak economy was pushed in certain directions by the government. In historical perspective, the Czechoslovak economy was one of the most tightly controlled capitalist systems in interwar Europe. From the very beginning, strict foreign currency regulations were enforced and they were only relaxed during the short economic boom between 1928 and 1931. The influence of important agrarian interests made it a political necessity for the government to increase the level of protection for numerous agricultural products (see Table 4.2). Although this led to the

Table 4.1: Government expenditure and revenue in Czechoslovakia, 1919–38 (in kč millions)

Year	Budget (estimate) Expenditure	Revenue	±	Final balance Expenditure	Revenue	±
1919	8,615	3,710	−4,905	7,449	4,736	−2,713
1920	11,604	7,804	−3,800	13,932	13,455	− 477
1921	18,026	17,299	− 727	18,557	20,725	+2,168
1922	19,813	18,884	− 929	20,496	18,711	−1,785
1923	19,371	18,812	− 559	18,287	16,619	−1,668
1924	16,994	16,391	− 603	18,544	18,008	− 536
1925	9,573	9,301	− 272	11,157	10,939	− 218
1926	9,710	10,086	+ 376	11,117	13,470	+2,353
1927	9,704	9,724	+ 20	10,536	10,455	− 81
1928	9,536	9,562	+ 26	11,340	9,981	−1,359
1929	9,534	9,570	+ 36	9,889	10,799	+ 910
1930	9,367	9,420	+ 53	9,873	9,647	− 226
1931	9,839	9,844	+ 5	11,102	9,133	−1,969
1932	9,319	9,323	+ 4	9,550	8,367	−1,183
1933	8,633	8,634	+ 1	9,082	7,575	−1,507
1934	7,631	7,632	+ 1	8,197	7,492	− 705
1935	7,983	7,985	+ 2	8,710	7,054	−1,656
1936	8,032	8,033	+ 1	9,314	7,554	−1,760
1937	8,454	8,456	+ 2	8,961	8,970	+ 9
1938	10,117	10,120	+ 3	−	−	−

Source: *Statistická ročenka*, relevant years.

Table 4.2: Duties on important agrarian commodities in Czechoslovakia, 1927–31

(1913 = Austro-Hungarian duties) Goods	1913	(in % of prices) 1927	1931
Wheat	36.8	16.5	89.5
Rye	34.8	20.5	104.0
Wheat flour	57.0	25.0	127.0
Pigs	2.5–37.0	2.7–10.2	15.1–87.0
Cauliflower	Duty free	21.6	40.0
Fresh pork	33.0	14.8–24.8	102.0
Raw sugar	21.5	133.0	366.0
Raw tobacco	91.5	228.0	340.0

Source: H. Liepmann, *Tariff levels and the economic unity of Europe* (London, 1938), p. 84.

partial loss of some traditional markets in South-east Europe, the basic policy to achieve an active balance of payments through a surplus of exports was adhered to consistently between 1920 and 1937 (see Table 3.16).

In general, the volume of public finance in Czechoslovakia was comparable to that of the leading industrial nations in Europe and accounted for one-fifth to one-third of the gross national product between 1920 and 1937. In distinction to the other countries, official expenditures by the Czechoslovak state on goods, services, subsidies for private and public companies, employment schemes, bank-rate reductions and export credits began to increase from 1930. In other words, in 1931 and 1932, the Czechoslovak government followed a policy of deficit financing which, despite the lack of a theoretical base, was capable in practice of reducing the shock of the economic crisis. However, this situation was not permitted to prevail because, as a result of the first and only catastrophic trade deficit in 1932, as well as irrational fears of inflationary developments, the government promptly returned to its balanced-budget policy and cut back public spending. With this change of direction in fiscal policy, the export-led crisis deepened and lengthened and, despite the much greater increase in government expenditures to accelerate rearmament and boost the economy from 1935 (see Table 4.3), deeply shook the economy, as well as the

Table 4.3: Defence expenditure in Czechoslovakia, 1935–8 (in kč milliards)

	1935	1936	1937	1938
I Ordinary budget				
Total expenditure	10,098	12,433	8,454	10,117
Total defence expenditure	2,692	3,761	1,793	4,449
of which administrative budget of the Ministry of Defence	1,289	1,509	1,348	2,087
of which special requirements for national defence	1,393	2,239	0,238	2,360
II Extraordinary budget (incomplete estimates)				
Public expenditure		6,828	4,124	5,408
of which civilian expenditure		0,923	0,830	0,646
of which military expenditure		5,905	3,294	4,762
III Other estimates of extraordinary expenditure			5,100	3,500

Source: M. Hauner, 'Military budgets and the armaments industry', *Papers in East European Economics*, 36 (Oxford, 1973), p. 45.

security of the independent republic. And it proved impossible to stop this trend despite two devaluations.

When England left the gold standard in 1931, the exchange rate of the pound fell by 31 per cent and, as the United States followed suit in 1933, the dollar initially lost 41 per cent in value. During this time, Czechoslovakia remained in the French-led gold block and lost its favourable position in the world market. As the pressure from the desperate situation in the export sector forced a devaluation in February 1934, the gold content of the crown was reduced by 16.7 per cent which only led to a brief recovery of foreign trade. Step by step, the gold block countries devalued their currencies and, in unison with them, Czechoslovakia followed with a 30 per cent devaluation in October 1936. Consequently, the price of Czechoslovak goods fell on the world market and prices on the domestic market began to increase more quickly than incomes. In conjunction with this development, the cautiously expansive policy mentioned above had a supportive impact on the economy. Nevertheless, throughout the 1930s, Czechoslovak exports and employment levels failed to regain the high level reached during the boom of 1929.

Public indebtedness

From the very beginning of the Czechoslovak Republic and throughout its existence the government, the town councils, large industrial enterprises and banks contracted long-term loans from abroad and frequently political as well as economic considerations played a significant role.

During the waves of revolution in Europe following the October Revolution in Russia and the First World War the British government provided the Czechoslovak state with a long-term credit for the purchase of food, which was to allay the unrest increased by lack of food supplies. Even German banks seeking credit abroad themselves provided short-term loans to enable the Czechoslovak government to buy food. These were soon repaid by the Czechoslovak government with sugar exports. However, the Czechoslovak government was not prepared to accept long-term loans from Germany, as on the one hand its political orientation was towards the Western Powers and on the other hand Germany was not, at that time, in a strong position to provide large long-term credits.

The ruling circles of both Czechoslovakia and the Western democracies were interested in building a strong army in Central Europe for a variety of military tasks within and beyond the frontiers of Czechoslovakia. The French military command in particular saw in the Czechoslovak army an ally not only against the Soviet Union but also against France's potential enemy, a revived Germany. France therefore extended a government loan to Czechoslovakia for military purposes and at the same time intervened directly with military and political support. According to the Franco-Czechoslovak Treaty of 1918, signed by the Czechoslovak Foreign Minister Dr Beneš, the Czechoslovak army became an integral part of the French army. The Head of the French Military Mission in Czechoslovakia, General Pellé, was appointed Chief of the General Staff of the Czechoslovak army in 1920; he was later replaced by General Mittelhauser, who held the post until 1925 when command was taken over by the Czechoslovak authorities. Further loans for military purposes were provided by the United States and by Britain, in connection with the upkeep and the repatriation of Czechoslovak legionaries in Siberia.

As a result of the Peace Treaty of Versailles the new Czechoslovak state was burdened with the greater part of the indebtedness of the former Austro-Hungarian monarchy. It was also decided that Czechoslovakia should pay into the reparation account the value of the former Austrian Emperor's family property taken over by the new state. In addition the Successor States were charged with a 'liberation tribute' of 1.5 milliard gold francs, of which Czechoslovakia in spite of her protests was to pay half as the economically and financially strongest. The whole question of Czechoslovakia's financial commitments to the Entente powers came under review during the Reparation Conference at the Hague in 1930. There representatives of the Czechoslovak government entered into a new agreement to pay regular instalments of 10 million gold francs annually for 37 years.

In 1922 the Czechoslovak government issued an investment loan in Britain and in the United States, which had a good reception in London and New York in spite of strong German competition. In many respects the situation was similar in Germany and in Czechoslovakia in the 1920s, with disrupted industry and relatively low wages attracting foreign investment.

Table 4.4: Statement of government debts of the Czechoslovak Republic, 1 January 1938 (from the budget for 1938)

Item Specification	Interest %	1 January 1938	Total in kč
1 Political debts: Arising out of the First World War and immediately after it. On the one hand credits from:			
USA	3.5	$115,000,000	
Britain	5	£ 401,491	
France	3	kč 254,688,056	
Italy	5	kč 472,258,351	
On the other hand the Liberation Debt	6	kč 335,401,315	5,720,547,313
2 Commitments to the Caisse Commune in Paris: Part of the debt of the former Austro-Hungarian monarchy which the Czechoslovak state took over according to the peace treaties	6		1,336,899,584
3 Actual foreign debt: Loans negotiated by the Czechoslovak government abroad: gold loan of ČSR in USA and Britain in 1922	8	kč 466,454,520	
Loan of ČSR in France of 1937 (conversion loan of 600 million frs. of 1932)	5	kč 697,674,000	1,164,128,520
Czechoslovak foreign debt total			8,251,575,417
Foreign debt amounts to 17.5 per cent of total Czechoslovak debt			47,094,386,474

Source: A. Teichova, *An economic background to Munich International business and Czechoslovakia* (Cambridge, 1974), p. 374.

The Czechoslovak state pledged as securities for their loans the income from customs and taxes and from the state monopolies of tobacco and saccharin. Thus the financial policy of the state was significantly influenced by its foreign indebtedness and was tied to that of the creditor states.

The most powerful creditor of the Czechoslovak state was the USA, providing 70 per cent of the total public foreign loans. The pre-Munich republic of Czechoslovakia belonged to those debtors of the United States which paid the highest rate of interest — at that time 8¾ per cent.

The relative importance of the main creditor countries which provided the Czechoslovak government with long-term loans remained essentially unchanged until 1938, as is shown in Table 4.4. In the 1930s investment slackened as a result of the general development of the international economy. Between 1929 and 1939 the United States limited its long-term credits primarily to its own domestic market and directed its foreign investments mainly to Canada and the Argentine. British investments flowed almost exclusively into the British Empire, and France also gave preference to her own colonies, although trying to retain her credit relations with European countries.

Czechoslovakia was considered the most solvent country in Central and South-east Europe. This is strikingly demonstrated by the figures in Table 4.4 where at the beginning of the fateful year of 1938 Czechoslovakia's foreign debt amounted to 17.5 per cent of the state's total indebtedness. Indeed, during the entire existence of the pre-Munich republic its internal indebtedness exceeded its external debt considerably whereas in the neighbouring Successor States foreign debts were chronically greater than domestic debts. In spite of this, however, particularly after Hitler's rise to power in Germany, investors preferred to provide the ČSR with short-term loans and tried to avoid entering into new long-term engagements. The exception was the long-term loan to the Czechoslovak state by France of kč 600 million in 1932, which was converted to kč 697,674,000 in 1937 (see Table 4.4) with an issue of 92 per cent and a rate of interest of 5 per cent. The French loan of 1937 is notable because it was primarily designed to save the Škoda Works. Obviously, the loan of 1932 and its conversion in 1937 were designed to strengthen French influence in Czechoslovakia.

Besides the French government loan, some long-term loans were granted to Czechoslovak big business by British creditors in the 1930s, but in comparison with the preceding period, lending from governments and private sources in the United States, Britain and France decreased although it never ceased entirely. In this field of economic relations also, Czechoslovakia remained in the sphere of Anglo-American-French interest.

SOCIAL POLICY

An important aspect of the demands for democratisation and radical economic and social reforms in Czechoslovakia was the general need felt by the bulk of the population for a comprehensive social insurance system supported by the state. Although significant progress had been made in this direction compared with the pre-war years, the Czechoslovak government developed no long-term concept for social investment in line with the requirements of constant economic growth and a continuous improvement in living standards. Essentially carried out under the influence of great political pressure, its social policy consisted of little more than relief campaigns, emergency measures and approving certain charitable organisations.

As in the other Successor States, defence had priority in the Czechoslovak budget above all other claims. Table 4.5 compares the budgetary allocations for education and public health with those for defence between 1925 and 1938. Whereas expenditures on social measures were higher than military expenditures at the end of the 1920s, the position was reversed by a significant

Table 4.5: Comparative expenditure on public health, education and defence in Czechoslovakia, 1925–38 (in kč milliards and in %)

Years	A Total expenditure	B Public health and education	C Defence[1]	B as % of A	C as % of A
1925	12,291		1,971		15.6
1929	10,275	2,412	1,792	23.4	17.0
1936	12,433	3,110	3,761	25.1	30.0
1938	10,117	3,164	4,499	31.3	40.4

Note: [1] Frontier guard and gendarmerie included in defence budget.
Source: Calculated from M. Hauner, 'Comparative social infrastructure and education in Eastern Europe' and 'Military budgets and the armaments industry', *Papers in East European Economics*, 26 and 36 (Oxford, 1973).

margin in the 1930s, reflecting the Czechoslovak reaction to the increasing aggressiveness of National Socialist Germany. In 1936, the government introduced an extraordinary budget to relieve the situation caused by the crisis and to finance employment creation through the Ministry for Public Works. A large part of these allocations were absorbed by the rearmament programme between 1936 and 1938.

As described above, Czechoslovakia carried out the most successful reform of schools and education of any country in Central and South-eastern Europe (see p. 15). However, public health and social welfare lagged behind the properly planned and executed measures in the field of education.

Czechoslovakia took over and expanded the Austro-Hungarian system of compulsory social insurance which had been introduced in Bohemia and Moravia in 1888 and in Slovakia in 1907. The system encompassed old-age pensions, invalidity, accident and medical insurance, as well as maternity and death benefits. However, the administration of the welfare and the medical insurance was distributed among a large number of different institutions and the services and benefits varied considerably. In the 1930s, various organisations were unified under the Central Social Insurance Institute, which concentrated mainly on the health service, and the General Pension Institute, which administered the old-age pensions, in Prague.

Under the pressure of the revolutionary wave of 1918–19, the Czechoslovak government introduced a general scheme of unemployment assistance which was transferred to the Ghent system with the new welfare legislation of 1924. This affected only unionised workers. In 1933, when there were almost 1 million registered unemployed, only a quarter of this number benefited from the state's contributions of 50 per cent to the payment of unemployment benefits through the Ghent system which the trade unions half financed and completely administered. Although Czechoslovakia was the most industrialised country of Central Europe and had the largest trade-union movement with 1,994,000 organised workers and salaried employees in 1934, the Ghent system of unemployment assistance only covered approximately one-third of all those out of work during the 1930s. Accordingly, the desperate situation of those completely impoverished people out of work could only be eased by the official food vouchers (*žebračenka* — beggars' ticket), various public job creation schemes and the work of various charities. In the last years of the pre-Munich republic, with their existence being increasingly endangered, unemployed men were drafted into defence work and public works on barracks; airfields, roads and railways were financed in Slovakia. Plans were also laid for relocating arms factories in the eastern region of the country. However, all this came too late either to save the republic or eliminate unemployment, to say nothing of reducing the backwardness of Slovakia in comparison with the Czech Lands.

In general, the Czechoslovak policy of free-market economics meant that Slovakia was subjected to the full force of capitalist competition and that, although its agricultural sector was able to keep up with overall developments, it stagnated in comparison with the western part of the country. Furthermore, in comparison with the Hungarian period when it was supported by legislation for the promotion of industry, Slovakia's industry changed very little during the interwar years. However, the government's social policy, in particular the school reforms and the democratisation of political life in Czechoslovakia, eliminated the effects of compulsory Magyarisation and contributed to the accelerated acquisition of their national identity among the Slovak people. At the same time, the provision of security for its citizens against the aggressive intentions of its neighbours was one of the main tasks of this joint state of Czechs and Slovaks.

The changes in the structure of the Czechoslovak economy sketched here took place against a background of increasing competition in Europe — particularly in South-east Europe — between West European and German financial interests which reached its peak on the eve of the Second World War. The most significant changes included: a relatively high degree of concentration; a shift in the relative weight of the consumer-goods industry compared with the production-goods industry; a reorientation of agricultural production; and upheaval in the territorial distribution and composition of the country's export goods. While these tendencies arose from the internal economic development in Czechoslovakia, external financial/political forces also influenced the economic life of the country: on the one hand, because, although small in comparison with its West European neighbours, the economy of Czechoslovakia was situated in an economically, politically and strategically important area and, on the other hand, because the Czechoslovak economy was largely dependent on foreign trade.

5

The Dismemberment of Czechoslovakia, 1938–45

International relations significantly influenced the establishment of the Republic of Czechoslovakia as an independent state in 1918 and did so again in 1938 when international events decisively contributed to the destruction of Czechoslovakia's independent statehood.

In 1938, the republic was the only surviving democracy in Central and South-east Europe. Since 1918, it had succeeded in building up the soundest economy of the states between Germany and the Soviet Union. During that time, as the industrially most advanced and economically strongest Successor State, Czechoslovakia had developed into a nodal point in relation to the economic interests of the Western powers in this area, as well as into a mediator between the economies of Western and Eastern Europe. Until the Munich Agreement — signed by Britain, France, Italy and Germany on 30 September 1938 — Czechoslovakia had belonged to the sphere of influence of Britain and France. As the balance of forces established after Versailles began to crumble during the world economic crisis, this country became the scene of increasingly complicated competitive struggles, in which Czechoslovak and German competition took place within the wider framework of entrenched West European positions, above all British and French, and the increasing efforts of Germany to achieve economic expansion and political revision in Central and South-east Europe. On the eve of the Second World War, international tensions reached a peak: the Anschluss of Austria on 11 March 1938 increased the threat to Czechoslovakia's independence from National Socialist Germany. As Czechoslovakia was the key to South-east Europe it is essential for the

understanding of the dramatic economic and political consequences of the Munich Agreement to refute the notion that,
long before the Munich Pact, there was a voluntary withdrawal
of West European and particularly British capital investment
from Central and South-east Europe, especially from Czechoslovakia. Up to the fateful meeting of the leading statesmen
of the four European powers — Chamberlain, Daladier,
Mussolini and Hitler — in Munich, no convincing evidence can
be found to support the hypothesis that Western direct foreign
investment had been withdrawn from Czechoslovakia in order
to facilitate the German economic advance into South-east
Europe. It was the Munich Agreement which broke all European political pacts and disrupted established economic links.

In the sphere of international capital investment Germany
made hardly any headway at all before 1938. As historical
evidence shows (see Chapter 3), German industrial companies and banks were unable to dislodge Britain and France,
and with them Czechoslovakia, from the leading positions in
South-east Europe even in the decade after regaining their
economic strength, that is between 1929 and the outbreak of the
Second World War.

In its drive for expansion, German capital sought to penetrate
the Czechoslovak economy in ways other than through direct
capital investment. In the first place, German business tried to
tie important Czechoslovak industrial enterprises to their own
by way of cartel agreements. The most influential German
cartels were able to make inroads into the trade of those industries in which British and French capital was strongly present
(see p. 46). Through cartels, German groups attempted to
gain greater influence in the economic life of Czechoslovakia
and thus to weaken the position of their British and French
competitors. In the second place, Hitler Germany's trade offen-
sive into South-east Europe endeavoured to undermine the
capital structure and political alliances which rested on the axis:
Britain and France in the West with Czechoslovakia as the
centre point linking them to South-east Europe.

By 1938, a wide gap had developed between the dominance
of Western finance and industry in the field of capital investment, on the one side, and the rising share of German trade in
the area of South-east Europe, on the other. However, German
economic policy of expansion was kept in limits. Hardly any
spectacular advances were made in the field of investments.

Only the violent intervention after Munich, followed by dismemberment of Czechoslovakia and the attack on Poland, changed the relation of forces between Western and German capital holdings in Central and South-east Europe. Within the international cartel mechanism, German business competed for higher production quotas and a larger share in the Central and South-east European markets. However, Czechoslovak cartel partners frequently blocked German advances by acting as a go-between for the stronger partners in international cartels from Britain and France. In general, German demands in international cartel negotiations were not met to their satisfaction before Munich. In addition, Germany's trade drive into South-east Europe as part of her *Grossraumwirtschaft* (greater German economy) plans did not lead to German dominance in that region before the destruction of the Czechoslovak economy. Nevertheless, under the special circumstances of depressed trade conditions of the 1930s, bilateral trade agreements between Germany and the weaker agrarian economies of South-east Europe succeeded in substantially increasing Germany's share in the foreign trade of these countries, thus drawing them more effectively into the German sphere of influence. As it became more obvious that German trade domination would ever more limit the economic room for manouevre of the South-east European states, they tried to extricate themselves from the German trade ensnarement and appealed to Britain for support.

Although Britain had comparatively less interest in Central and South-east Europe than in its traditional areas of economic activity, that is, the British Empire and Latin America, and despite the fact that, in the spirit of appeasement, the Chamberlain government was prepared to accept a certain strengthening of German economic influence in this area, British readiness to make concessions was accompanied by a demand for safeguards for the country's own interests in the Danubian region. Thus a bargain was struck with Hitler on the basis of the sacrifice of Czechoslovak independence and the prospect of maintaining Western, mainly British interests. Far-reaching economic adjustments between Britain and Germany were to take place after Munich.

However, in the aftermath of the Munich Agreement, Hitler Germany proceeded to achieve demands by force. Changes in the structure of capital investment, of the cartel system and of trade relations in favour of Germany followed the British and

French surrender in Munich, as well as the conquest of Europe by the Third Reich during the Second World War.

In the very short period between 1 October 1938 and 15 March 1939, Czechoslovakia was dismembered, her economy rent asunder, and her role in the international economy eliminated.

The various parts of her formerly integrated economy were destined to serve the German war economy. According to the conditions agreed at Munich, those Czechoslovak areas along the German border with a 50 per cent German-speaking population were to be incorporated into the German Reich. In this way, Czechoslovakia was also to be served up to Germany militarily, for her frontiers with Germany had been secured by fortifications built according to the latest French technology on the model of the Maginot Line. On the very day of the signing of the Munich Agreement, Poland demanded the highly industrialised region of Těšín and, on the next day, Hungary claimed a certain area of southern Slovakia and the Carpatho-Ukraine. The Prague government had to yield to these demands, although 1,500,000 Czechs, Slovaks and Ukrainians lived in these areas and, suddenly, as a result of these annexations, found themselves living as minority groups in Poland or Hungary. Many thousands streamed into the Czech, Moravian or Slovak interior to escape the surrounding fascist dictatorships.

After the loss of 30 per cent of her territory, a third of her population and two-fifths of her industrial capacity, the Rump Czechoslovakia — the so-called Second Republic — survived just under half a year. On 15 March 1939 German troops occupied the western areas which were incorporated into the Third Reich as the 'Protectorate of Bohemia and Moravia'. Even before this, at the beginning of October 1938, Slovakia had declared herself as an autonomous part of the Second Republic and on 14 March 1939 it was constituted as a vassal of Hitler's Germany, formally as an independent Slovak state.

Pre-Munich Czechoslovakia was torn into five pieces, each of which developed peculiarly in different economic units. Of the total industrial production of former Czechoslovakia 70 per cent was accounted for by the 'Protectorate of Bohemia and Moravia', 22 per cent by the frontier areas which, between Munich and the end of the war, were known as the 'Sudetenland', and 8 per cent by Slovakia.

The 'Protectorate' was most important for the German war

production because it included the largest share of total production of the Czechoslovak iron and steel, metal and machine industries, while the 'Sudetenland' had a relatively larger share of the output of textiles and other consumer goods industries. During the years from 1941 to 1944 the Czech regions were of particular value to the German armament industry as places of greater security from Allied air bombardment. According to estimates based on the number of persons employed, the region of Bohemia and Moravia contributed 9–12 per cent to the total of greater Germany's industrial production during the war years. This share was relatively greater than the share of any other region of the Third Reich, despite the fact that productivity declined in those years. In accordance with the aims of National Socialist expansion, Bohemia and Moravia were regarded as colonies which provided Germany with industrial enterprises, with military and financial resources and workers. Similarly *Arisierung* (Aryanisation) — the confiscation of Jewish property, which was regarded as war booty — served the same purpose.

The Slovak state came into existence under the protection of Hitler's Germany and was incorporated into the greater German economy (*Grossraumwirtschaft*). This meant, above all, the transfer of the greater part of the Slovak industrial, transport and commercial companies into German hands: the share of German participation in the total Slovak joint-stock capital grew from 0.2 per cent to 62 per cent between 1939 and 1945, while the Czech share decreased from 84 per cent to 8 per cent and the Slovak share increased only from 15 per cent to 18 per cent. However, the number employed in industry rose by 50 per cent in comparison with 1939 as a result of the needs of the war economy, although the so-called German-Slovak Protection Agreement only permitted the establishment of new industrial enterprises with German approval. In many cases permission was not granted by the Germans and the development of Slovak industrialisation was channelled into agricultural production, raw material processing and especially into the procurement of timber.

The Slovak population, in comparison with that of the occupied Czech territory, participated to a greater extent in the 'Aryanisation' of Jewish property and the 'Slovakisation' of Czech property. This concerned mainly small to medium-sized enterprises and shops in commerce and trades. It was the

Figure 5.1: The dismemberment of Czechoslovakia, 1938–9

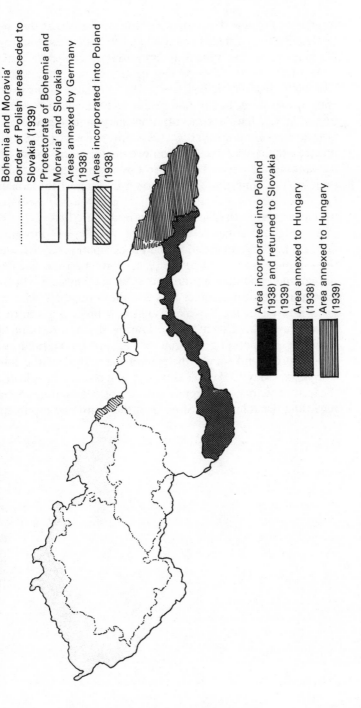

— ⋅ — ⋅ — Border of 'Protectorate of Bohemia and Moravia'

⋯⋯⋯⋯⋯ Border of Polish areas ceded to Slovakia (1939)

☐ 'Protectorate of Bohemia and Moravia' and Slovakia

☐ Areas annexed by Germany (1938)

▨ Areas incorporated into Poland (1938)

■ Area incorporated into Poland (1938) and returned to Slovakia (1939)

▓ Area annexed to Hungary (1938)

▥ Area annexed to Hungary (1939)

tragedy of the Jewish population of these areas that they were firstly deprived of their livelihood and then delivered up to the Germans to be annihilated in concentration camps.

As a trade partner, Slovakia became a substantial creditor of Germany. Slovakia never received full payment for its exports and, furthermore, had to find resources to finance the deportation of Slovak Jews to concentration camps and to pay wages to Slovak workers employed in Germany. In addition Slovakia financed the cost of the German occupation of its country and its war with the Soviet Union. All this expenditure led to inflation. At the same time, opposition grew against the domestic fascist regime, as well as against German National Socialism, which erupted in the Slovak Rising in August 1944.

Although the armed resistance in Slovakia was suppressed by German military intervention and the occupation of Slovakia by the German army in October 1944, active partisan units held out in the mountainous area of Central Slovakia until the breakthrough of the Soviet Army in the spring of 1945.

As a result of the Slovak Rising, new life was given to the resistance in the Czech Lands. During the first days of May 1945, the population of Prague rose against the German occupation forces and fought them until the arrival of the Soviet troops on 9 May 1945. The Slovak Rising powerfully influenced the further history of the renewed Czechoslovak state, especially regarding the role of the Slovaks in the reinstated republic.

Part 2

Czechoslovakia after the Second World War

6

The Preconditions for Reconstruction after the Second World War

Following the total defeat of National Socialist Germany, the Czechoslovak state was recreated within its pre-Munich borders, with the exception of the Carpatho-Ukraine which was ceded to the Soviet Union on 29 June 1945. The liberation of Czechoslovakia started with the Slovak uprising against the German army in August 1944. On the harsh road to the restoration of an independent Czechoslovak Republic, the Slovak uprising played a decisive role. Its long-term repercussions can be ranked with two other historic events which considerably affected the socio-political life of post-1945 Czechoslovakia. The first event concerns the complete elimination of the population and the erasure of the town of Lidice by the German occupation authority in the 'Protectorate of Bohemia and Moravia' on June 10 1942. This atrocity created a storm of horror and indignation in the countries of the Allies and contributed significantly to the annulment of the Munich Agreement of 30 September 1938 by its Western signatories. The second event is connected with the May Rising against the German occupiers in Prague where fighting lasted until 9 May 1945 — a day after V-Day, the official ending of the war in Europe.

On 5 April 1945, after the return of the President of the Republic, Dr Eduard Beneš, to the liberated area, the programme of the new Government of the National Front of Czechs and Slovaks was published in the East Slovak city of Košice. It affirmed the equal standing of Czechs and Slovaks in the joint state.

In general, although the economic orientation of post-war governments in Central and South-east Europe was not directly dictated by the Soviet Army, it was certainly decisively influenced by its presence. This applies to Czechoslovakia too. However, for specific historical reasons, it held a special position as the industrially most advanced state in Central and South-east Europe. Czechoslovakia was able to make an immediate start on a constructive policy of reconstruction because, through intensive negotiations about major foreign and domestic issues, the Czechoslovak government in exile was able to prevent serious differences arising. Accordingly, as President of Czechoslovakia in Exile, Eduard Beneš succeeded in obtaining the agreement of the four allied powers (the United States, Britain, France and the Soviet Union) to his main policies: in particular, to the complete annulment of the Munich Agreement, to the conclusion of the Czechoslovak–Soviet Alliance signed in 1943, and to the compulsory resettlement of the German population from the new Czechoslovak Republic.

From a foreign political point of view, there was a great deal of sympathy in Czechoslovakia for the Soviet Union and its putatively more equitable social system because the Soviets were not only regarded as liberators from the horrors of Nazi occupation but also as friends due to their rejection of the Munich Agreement in 1938 and, following the conclusion of the Czechoslovak–Soviet Alliance in December 1943, as protectors of the independence of the reborn state. The withdrawal of the Soviet Army from Czechoslovakia in November 1945 strengthened this trust. Furthermore, friendly contacts were to be maintained with the Slav nations and, in particular, with the Western Powers. However, this foreign policy was based on the assumption of a harmonious relationship between East and West.

As far as domestic politics were concerned, the reborn Czechoslovak Republic — which, on the basis of the national and democratic revolution, was a people's democracy between 1945 and 1948 — started life under a relatively favourable political constellation. During the last phase of the war, an agreement was reached between the government in exile in London under Eduard Beneš and the *émigré* leaders of the Czechoslovak communists in Moscow under Klement Gottwald which enjoyed the support of the various resistance groups in their homeland. Hence, it was possible for them to prepare a joint policy for the interim National Front government based on the Košice Programme.

In the field of social and economic policy, the main results of this co-operation were the confiscation of property belonging to the enemy, war criminals, traitors and collaborators and the management of the confiscated property by officially nominated administrative bodies. Of enduring significance was the nationalisation of key industries, including banking and insurance. Simultaneously, easier access to credit facilities was promised for small and medium-sized enterprises and tradesmen. A prominent position was given to the land reform programme which aimed to satisfy the demands of landless and small peasants. These measures enjoyed the support of numerous segments of the population. In addition, following the dramatic experiences of the economic crisis and the fascist war economy, there was a widespread belief among both Czechs and Slovaks of the necessity for socialist reforms and the need to contain the negative aspects of the capitalist free-market economy by state control. Although no consensus existed with regard to the methods of economic planning to be employed, there was a clear preference for the concept of an economic and financial democracy which would have given broad social groups rights of co-determination in the decision-making processes on the course of production and consumption.

The nationalities policy of the interim National Front government was securely anchored in the Košice Programme and guaranteed equality between Czechs and Slovaks. There was general acceptance of the policy of compulsory resettlement of Germans from Czechoslovakia, as well as the exchange of the Hungarian minority against Slovaks living in Hungary.

Within the National Front government, despite a variety of ideas about implementation, there was general agreement with respect to the main directions of the immediate policy of political, social, economic and national reconstruction. At this time, the National Front was a pluralistic, democratic coalition of parties — the Communist Party of Czechoslovakia (KSČ), the Czech Social Democratic Party (ČSDP), the Czechoslovak Socialist Party (ČSP), the People's Party, the Commmunist Party of Slovakia (KSS) and the Slovak Democratic Party — and diverse interest groups — trade unions, co-operatives, youth and resistance-fighter organisations, etc. — excluding those who had been exposed as collaborators. Since 1941, the Communist Party had acquired great authority in the resistance movement and, with the end of the war, enjoyed the broad support of the workers, peasants and intellectuals. While the party's long-term objective remained the achievement of a

Soviet-style system, it followed a policy, 'of the specific Czechoslovak way to Socialism', which was to be followed hand in hand with the developing national and democratic revolution. This approach to the solution of the backlog of problems arising from the occupation and war was supported by a majority of the population.

The first — and last — free democratic elections to be held after the war on 26 May 1946 confirm the singular degree of consensus existing at this time with the communists emerging as the strongest party.[1] The General Secretary of the Communist Party, Klement Gottwald, was appointed Prime Minister to head the new government of the National Front which reflected the result of the election and held office until February 1948. It stuck to the basic principles of the Košice Programme and continued with the process of converting it into reality. At the end of 1946, the new government adopted the 'Two-Year Plan for the Renewal and Reconstruction of the Czechoslovak Economy'.

With the implementation of the two-year plan, Czechoslovakia became the second country after the Soviet Union to take the path of a planned economy. However, it was the first highly industrialised country ever to introduce into a democratic political society a system of central economic guidance which took into account market conditions. In this respect, too, Czechoslovakia held a special position among the planned economies of Central and South-east Europe, including the Soviet Union, because the relative economic backwardness of these states forced them to apply a strict system of centralised planning and control. In distinction to these countries, Czechoslovakia was able to draw on an advanced production apparatus, on a highly developed system of trade and commerce, relatively progressive industrial and agricultural sectors, as well as substantial reserves of technically, scientifically and generally well-educated workers, during the transition period to a system of economic guidance.

The following chapters discuss how Czechoslovakia was able to make use of this favourable starting position. At this point, mention need only be made of the fact that, within less than a decade, the two-year plan and the subsequent five-year plan had not only led to profound economic change, but also to the most radical social restructuring in Czechoslovak history.

NOTES

1. Results of the Election of 26 May 1946 (in per cent): KSČ and KSS, 38 per cent (in the Czech Lands, 40.2 per cent); ČSDP, 12.8 per cent; ČSP, 18.3 per cent; People's Party, 15.6 per cent; Democratic Party, 14.1 per cent (in Slovakia, 62 per cent, KSS, 30.4 per cent).

7

Population — from a Multinational to a Binational State

STRUCTURE, GROWTH AND DENSITY OF POPULATION

Between 1945 and 1950, the population structure changed dramatically compared with 1937 and Czechoslovakia became basically a binational state of Czechs and Slovaks.

According to the first post-war census in 1950, the territory of the state had shrunk to 127,870 square kilometres through the cession of the Carpatho-Ukraine to the USSR. This meant that the economically most backward part of the republic had been separated off from the relatively advanced western regions. At the same time, the total population fell by 2,899,846 to 12,338,100 compared with 1937 (see Table 1.1). Apart from the major decline as a result of the war, between 1938 and 1948, the main cause of this drop in numbers was the massive compulsory resettlement of the German minority (see p. 96). As shown in Tables 1.1 and 1.4, the greatest impact was felt in the Czech Lands where the population density in 1950 had fallen to the level of 1900 and did not regain the 1937 level until well into the 1970s. Taking the country as a whole, it was not until 1980 that the population reached 15,283,000 and thus slightly exceeded that of 1937. On the other hand, there was both an absolute and a relative increase in the population of Slovakia, with the percentage of Slovaks climbing from 23.2 per cent in 1937 to 27.9 in 1950 and 32 per cent in 1980. In addition, the population density in Slovakia also rose in line with the accelerated process of industrialisation from 72 per square kilometre in 1930 to 101 in 1980.

The relatively rapid population growth in Slovakia is reflected in the statistics of the natural population increase of the post-war years and is shown in comparison with that of the pre-Munich republic in Table 1.2. In general, the natural population movements in Czechoslovakia between 1945 and 1950 differed only insignificantly from those of other industrial countries with a considerable initial rate of growth which then begins to fall off sharply, despite the reduction in child mortality between 1947 and 1969. Since the middle of the 1950s, there has been an absolute drop in the number of live births and, at the same time as the fall in the fertility rate, a dramatic increase in the number of abortions following its legalisation in 1957 (from 2.8 per 1,000 inhabitants in 1956 to an average of 8.5 per 1,000 between 1957 and 1970). Above all else, this negative demographic development emanated from the inclusion of an extremely high proportion of women in the working population and from worsening social conditions, especially from a serious shortfall of housing.

Naturally, the age structure of the population did not remain unchanged. Following the resettlement of the relatively aged German minority and the initial sharp rise in the birth rate, there was a drop in the average age of the population. However, this held true only until 1955 when regressive development trends began to appear. According to data published by the Statistical Office of the Federal Republic of Czechoslovakia, between 1950 and 1970, the proportion of people of pensionable age (men over 60 and women over 55) rose from 14.4 to 19.6 per cent while the age group up to 14 fell from 25.4 to 23.9 per cent and the share of people of productive age (men aged 15–59 and women aged 15–54) slipped from 60.2 to 56.5 per cent. At the same time, there was also an increase in average life expectancy.

MIGRATION AND CHANGES IN THE NATIONALITY STRUCTURE

The Second World War in Europe led to population movements of staggering dimensions. Czechoslovakia, where migration took place in various phases, was not excepted from this.

The government's repatriation campaign began immediately the war ended and resulted in around 950,000 people returning to their homeland by the end of September 1948. Of these, some 800,000 were Czechoslovak citizens who had been transported to National Socialist Germany as forced labour, as well as concentration camp survivors who had survived the fate of another 235,000 prisoners murdered by the Nazis. The total figure also includes soldiers who had fought abroad in the ranks of the Czechoslovak units. A further 150,000 returned from political and economic exile.

The most significant factor leading to a radical change in the nationalities structure of the population was the compulsory resettlement of the German minority from Czechoslovakia. Carried out systematically, the actions of the Czechoslovak government were based on a decision taken by the victorious allied powers at the Potsdam Conference (17 July to 2 August 1945). Officially, the process of expulsion began on 25 January 1946 and was more or less completed by November 1946, although the official end was not until mid-1947. In this period, a total of 2,996,000 Germans were resettled with the loss of their Czechoslovak citizenship and their property, except personal belongings. Of this number, 176,000 came from Slovakia, and 660,000 people of German nationality had left Czechoslovakia before the official campaign had started. Approximately 150,000 Germans were permitted to remain in the republic, above all specialists considered to be indispensible, anti-fascists and the spouses of mixed marriages.

A similar fate was in store for approximately half a million members of the Hungarian minority in Slovakia. Although this process started spontaneously, it was stopped in 1946 as a result of the Czechoslovak–Hungarian peace negotiations and infringements had to be remedied as far as possible. According to the treaty, a total of 68,407 Hungarians (approximately 12 per cent of the Hungarian minority) were to be exchanged for an equivalent number of Slovaks returning from Hungary.

Accordingly, the nationalities structure of Czechoslovakia had changed fundamentally by the time of the 1950 census. The most significant difference stemmed from the almost complete expulsion of the German minority which plummeted from 22.53 per cent of the total population in 1930 to 1.3 per cent in 1950 and, due to its age structure, disappeared altogether from the population statistics in the years that followed. The numbers of the other national minorities also fell significantly. The transformation of Czechoslovakia into a dual nationality state was the product of these population changes and, since the census of

1950, the population has basically consisted of about one-third Slovaks and two-thirds Czechs (see Table 1.3).

Two other, politically induced, emigration waves number among the most remarkable features of the post-war population statistics and, although they are by no means of the same magnitude as the compulsory resettlement policies, they left a noticeable mark on certain sections of society. According to official Czechoslovak statistics, a total of 10,685 citizens emigrated between 1948 and 1949. Because this must be considered a consequence of the accession to power of the communists in February 1948, it can be assumed that the overwhelming majority of this number were Czechs and Slovaks who were not in agreement with the new political constellation. Following the Soviet-led invasion of Czechoslovakia by the Warsaw Pact countries in August 1968, 31,769 people — a large proportion of them young people and intellectuals — emigrated between 1968 and 1970. In both cases, the emigration figures exceeded the average of the subsequent, restrictive years by three to five times. The last emigration wave is of particular significance due to its generally negative impact on the age structure of the population.

The hasty resettlement policy of 1946 led to a decisive loss of labour power and to depopulation in parts of the advanced agricultural areas and highly industrialised regions in the north and north-west of the country. This required an effective policy of domestic resettlement resulting in large population movements within Czechoslovakia. Although the influx came from almost all districts, there was a flood of people from the still relatively overpopulated rural areas of Slovakia who came to occupy land and jobs in the frontier regions. By the middle of 1946 some 2,000,000 — and by December 1948 2,590,149 — people had been resettled in the border regions of Czechoslovakia. Although this number was almost equal to that of the displaced population, the waste of resources, the low level of agricultural production and a lack of skilled workers meant that the economic efficiency of these regions could only be restored and put to good use after a great deal of time had been spent overcoming major difficulties. After 1950, the population movement from Slovakia to the Czech Lands continued with a further 161,000 people migrating there by 1969.

Parallel with this, the centrally planned industrialisation led to an increasing proportion of the population living in towns and cities (the percentage of the population living in communities with less than 2,000 inhabitants sank from 52.6 per cent in 1930 to 38 per cent in 1970) and to a concentration of population in urban areas. The impact of industrialisation is also reflected in the distribution of the gainfully employed population during the period of the socialist planned economy when the name Czechoslovak Socialist Republic (ČSSR) was officially adopted in 1960.

DISTRIBUTION OF THE ECONOMICALLY ACTIVE POPULATION

Table 3.8 illustrates the considerable restructuring which took place in the distribution according to economic sectors of the working population between 1950 and 1980. Its share in the industrial sector rose from 36.3 to 55.2 per cent and fell from 30.9 to 13.1 per cent in agriculture. In the tertiary sector, there was a slight decrease from 32.8 to 31.7 per cent. Compared with other similarly advanced capitalist economies in Europe, the Czechoslovak service sector lagged far behind. In the 25 years from 1945 to 1970, when the industrialisation of Slovakia was pushed ahead at high speed, the steepness of the west–east gradient of the pre-Munich republic was mitigated to a large extent so that the gap between Slovakia and the Czech Lands which, in 1948, had been estimated at more than 50 years, had been reduced to approximately 20 years by 1968.

The distribution, according to the main branches of the Czechoslovak economy, of the working population for 1968 is shown in Table 7.1. It presents the classification of the economy into productive and non-productive sectors in accordance with the Marxist concept — which holds that only the creation of material goods can be regarded as productive — and became an integral part of all macro-economic calculations of the ČSSR. To a certain extent, this also explains the neglect of the tertiary sector. Although the rates of growth for numbers employed in science and research, as well as in the social services, climbed visibly, the overwhelming majority of the working population remained in the industrial and building sectors. Furthermore, half of all people who had been employed in agricultural work in 1948 had left this sector by 1968, the majority of them finding work in industrial occupations.

Table 7.1: Occupational distribution among main sectors of the Czechoslovak economy, 1948 and 1968

Sector	1948	1968	Increase or decrease 1948–68		In % of total employed	
	(in thousands)		absolute	in %	1948	1968
Total employed	5,545	6,798	+1,253	22.6	100	100
out of this:						
Productive sector	4,842	5,358	+ 516	10.7	87.3	78.8
Industry	1,640	2,605	+ 965	58.8	29.6	38.3
Building	253	576	+ 323	127.7	4.5	8.5
Agriculture	2,239	1,211	−1,028	− 45.9	40.4	17.8
Forestry	92	103	+ 11	12.0	1.6	1.5
Transport	141	203	+ 62	44.0	2.5	3.0
Communication	26	47	+ 21	80.8	0.5	0.7
Commerce and						
public catering	370	499	+ 129	34.9	6.7	7.3
Unproductive sector	703	1,440	+ 737	104.8	12.7	21.2
Transport	87	148	+ 61	70.1	1.6	2.2
Communication	26	47	+ 21	80.8	0.5	0.7
Science and research	20	173	+ 153	765.0	0.3	2.5
Municipal services	73	162	+ 89	121.9	1.3	2.4
Health and social						
insurance	91	244	+ 153	168.1	1.6	3.6
Schools, culture,						
popularisation of						
learning, sport	138	407	+ 269	194.9	2.5	6.0
Administration						
and justice	137	111	− 26	− 19.0	2.5	1.6

Source: *25 let Československa,* p. 36.

By the end of the two-year plan in 1948, the Czechoslovak economy had roughly regained its pre-war level and full employment had been attained (see p. 121). In the subsequent planning periods, the total number of persons who had been sucked into paid employment — from all social groups — rose by 22.6 per cent between 1948 and 1968 (see Table 7.1). The resulting social levelling will be discussed in the following chapter. At this point, mention should only be made of the role played by women in this development, because they contributed most to the expansion of the number of employed persons: of the total increase of 1,602,000 workers between 1950 and 1972, 1,258,000 or 78.5 per cent were women. In the 1970s, the level of employment reached such a degree of intensity that any further rise in the number of male workers was considered impossible and a further increase in the number of women would have endangered the development of the population even more. A contradictory situation arose: on the one hand, the planners strove to employ an ever increasing number of workers in production; on the other hand, acting against the demands of the economy for more workers were the low retirement age, conscription, the swelling bureaucratic apparatus, the large number of young people in higher education and the social measures taken to boost the birth rate. Hence, in the productive sector, there is a declining trend in the rate of growth in the number of employed persons between 1971 and 1979, whereas there is an increasing trend in the non-productive sector (compare Table 9.1B, level of employment). Because the reserves of labour had been largely exhausted, any future increase in output could only be achieved by the general increase in productivity sought by planners.

8

Society — from a Bourgeois to an Egalitarian Society

In order to comprehend properly the fundamental structural changes which took place in Czechoslovak society, it is necessary to explain them in conjunction with the revolutionary interventions in property relationships between 1945 and 1953. In this short period of time, the basis of the capitalist social order was destroyed. The economic foundation of this transition phase from capitalism to socialism consisted of the nationalisation of all means of production so that finally only personal possessions remained in private hands.

The atmosphere in Czechoslovakia at this time was favourable for the introduction of such measures because the desire for greater equality had deep historical roots in the social consciousness of broad segments of society. The social changes during the war — particularly in the Czech Lands — encouraged these hopes even more because the social scale in Czechoslovakia was characterised, at the one end, by the collaboration of big business with the National Socialist occupiers and, at the other end, by the continuous uprooting and loss of social standing of the lower-bourgeoisie as a result of labour deployment at home and forced labour in Germany. Accordingly, the main claims of the KSČ, which were also supported by the Czechoslovak SPD, reflected the general mood of a population that was fully opposed to any policy of reprivatisation. At the same time, works councils were spontaneously elected in all industrial areas. These bodies pushed forward the socialisation of their factories. In some cases, they even took over control of their plants and it was not until the communists came to power in 1948 that, step by step, their economic and political influence was curtailed. It was under these objective conditions that Czechoslovakia became the first country after the Soviet Union to nationalise completely big business, banks and insurance companies.

SOCIAL CLASSES AND SOCIAL MOBILITY

In this way, the economic and, consequently, the political position of the bourgeoisie was substantially weakened during the first three post-war years. With the exception of only a few large enterprises that had adopted an anti-fascist attitude, Czechoslovak big business had adapted to the demands of the German war economy and, accordingly — together with the property of collaborators, traitors and war profiteers, as well as that of the enemy — was subject to immediate nationalisation without compensation in accordance with the Košice Programme. This was followed by the first major nationalisation wave between 1945 and 1947. On 24 October 1945, President Beneš signed the Nationalisation Decree, which was ceremoniously announced on 28 October, the anniversary of the foundation of the first Czechoslovak Republic in 1918. Whole branches of industry were affected by this move with key industries such as mining, electricity supply, iron and steel, armaments, the chemical and pharmaceutical industry, cellulose production, cement works, sugar refineries and distilleries, as well as all banks and insurance companies, being taken into public ownership. In other branches of industry, only enterprises with less than 500 employees could escape nationalisation, although, when considered to be in the national interest, this figure could fall as low as 150 or be measured in terms of production capacity. Thus, by the spring of 1947, nationalised industries and confiscated companies employed approximately 80 per cent of all workers and disposed of over two-thirds of Czechoslovakia's total production capacity. Although provision had been made for compensation in the nationalisation law, only foreign proprietors benefited from this possibility. In other words, all Czechoslovaks owning large companies emerged empty-handed. When the first nationalisation wave came to an end, the Czechoslovak economy consisted of a socialist sector and a sector of small private businesses and traders.

The Czechoslovak bourgeoisie suffered further severe blows in the aftermath of the first post-war currency reform on

1 November 1945 and the millionaires' levy in October 1947. Although the primary objective of the currency reform was to bring the wartime inflation to a stop and to stabilise the exchange rate of the Czechoslovak crown within the framework of the International Monetary Fund, the government restricted all citizens to only 500 crowns and withdrew 85 per cent of the money in circulation. In addition, all bank accounts, including savings accounts, were frozen with withdrawals only being released with special permission and all life insurances and government securities were frozen. The effect of these measures was to soak up both inflation money and accumulated war profits. As the political and economic situation worsened during 1947 (see p. 119), the KSČ insisted on a one-off property tax, the so-called millionaires' levy, which was expected to cover up to 50,000 people and bring in some kč 3 milliard ($20 million). After a major political controversy in Parliament, the millionaires' levy became law at the end of October 1947 and, as a result, the government's revenues increased by approximately kč 1.1 milliard. Although this was only a third of the anticipated amount, it nevertheless played a significant role in weakening the position of large property owners.

During this period of increased international and domestic tension, communist policy in Czechoslovakia was aimed at transferring political power step by step to the KSČ, as well as constantly expanding the public sector of the economy and placing increasing pressure on the private sector. In February 1948 the KSČ succeeded in exploiting the government crisis to its advantage and on 25 February the government was rebuilt under Klement Gottwald with communists in command of all major posts. With the law of 28 April 1948, the new government introduced the second nationalisation wave which took all enterprises with more than 50 employees into public ownership, as well as completely nationalising all aspects of the wholesale trade and foreign trade. In the first half of 1948 steps were taken to reorganise the banking system leaving only one bank in the Czech Lands and one in Slovakia. Additionally, the savings banks were nationalised and unified/managed. During 1948, the nationalisation campaign exceeded the statutory limits and, by the end of the year, almost all private companies employing more than 20 people had disappeared. Through the combined effect of all these measures, the bourgeoisie had the economic carpet pulled away from under them and a significant social force was eliminated. Their fate was sealed by the radical currency reform of 1 June 1953, in which all funds left in accounts blocked since the first currency reform, as well as all government securities, were annulled and every citizen was given a cash pay-off of 300 new crowns (see p. 139). In so far as they had not emigrated before 1948, the middle strata were integrated into the new system as workers and white-collar employees.

Small businesses and traders were not affected by the nationalisation waves between 1945 and 1948. On the contrary, the material situation of retailers, self-employed craftsmen and tradesmen was satisfactory thanks, on the one hand, to the rapid economic upswing and, on the other hand, to the chance of acquiring at favourable conditions confiscated workshops, factories and shops, as well as houses and other expropriated property, the bulk of which was located in the border areas of Czechoslovakia formerly populated by the German minority. This social mobility is difficult to quantify or classify due to a lack of statistical and sociological data. However, it can be assumed that this influx into the middle strata of society came primarily from urban proletariat or semi-proletariat groups. Nevertheless the period of upward social mobility was relatively short because, between 1948 and 1953, self-employed craftsmen and industrial producers were completely nationalised and, consequently, the petty bourgeoisie economically liquidated. With this radical intervention in the private, small business sector, the Czechoslovak nationalisation policy went beyond that of any other Central and South-east European country. Of the 383,000 small companies with 905,000 employed and self-employed workers in 1948, only 47,000 firms with 50,000 people remained in 1956. And this number diminished from year to year until 1972 when only 2,000 isolated self-employed craftsmen were left (see Table 8.1).[1]

Initially, social change among the agricultural population was the result of the post-war land reform implemented from 1945 to roughly 1951. Thereafter, it was accelerated by the process of collectivisation which completely negated the social and economic effects of the land reform and created a drastically different stratification of the agricultural population (see Table 8.1).

As mentioned in the introduction, the land reform ranked among the main priorities of the Košice Programme. Further-

Table 8.1: Social stratification of the Czechoslovak population, 1930–80 (in %)

Social Group	1930[1]	1950	1961	1970	1980	Growth/decline (in %)
Blue-collar workers	57.3	56.4	56.3	60.1	62.1	10.1
White-collar workers[3]	6.8	16.4	27.9	27.4	28.6	11.2
Peasants on collective farms	–	–	10.6	9.4	7.4	−16.2
Other members of productive co-operatives	–	–	1.2	1.7	1.5	− 3.7
Peasants (smallholders)	22.2	20.3	3.5	1.2	0.3	−77.5
Artisans, tradesmen	8.2	3.8	0.4	0.1	–	−33.3
Capitalist entrepreneurs and professions	5.5	3.1	0.1[2]	0.1[2]	0.1[2]	−30.3[2]

Notes:
[1] post-war territory.
[2] professions.
[3] After 1950 this category includes heterogeneous groups which developed a new hierarchical stratification (see p. 111).
Sources: *25 let Československa*, p. 7; *Statistická ročenka*, relevant years.

more, between 1945 and 1949, it held a similarly high position alongside the nationalisation of the industrial sector in the policy of the KSČ; because in the planned socialist society of Czechoslovakia the hunger of the agricultural population for land was to be satisfied and, thereby, programmatically mould the 'alliance of workers and peasants'. This is the main reason why the KSČ was able to count on significant support from the agricultural population in the elections of 1946.

The land reform was carried out in three stages. The first stage began spontaneously — in Slovakia in February 1945 and in the Czech Lands in May 1945 — with estates and peasants' holdings that had been confiscated during the occupation being taken back and land belonging to Germans and Hungarians being redistributed by revolutionary peasant commissions. With the decree of the President of the Republic of 21 June 1945, 'Concerning the Confiscation, Distribution and Settlement of Land of the Enemy and Traitors', the redistribution of arable land, forests and other property was continued on a statutory basis. This category covered approximately a quarter of the total area of the Republic of Czechoslovakia (2,946,395 hectares, of which 1,295,379 hectares was forest land). Of the total of 1.8 million hectares of arable land distributed to Czech and Slovak settlers, approximately 1.4 million hectares came primarily from former German agricultural holdings, as well as to a lesser extent from Hungarian holdings.

The second stage followed in July 1947. Its objective was to complete the unfinished land reform of the pre-Munich republic by adhering strictly to the expropriation of all estates (against compensation) in excess of 250 hectares and over 150 hectares of arable land (see p. 28). This process turned up another 800,000 hectares for redistribution via the Land Fund. In the central parts of the Czech Lands and in Slovakia, the total of arable land redistributed amounted to 100,000 hectares and 275,000 hectares respectively.

The third stage was actually carried out immediately after the communist accession to power. Designated 'new', this phase set the upper limit for private ownership at 50 hectares and resulted in the expropriation of a further 700,000 hectares, whereby by far the major part of this total was taken into state ownership and only a relatively small part given to landless and dwarf peasants.

The impact of the three land-reform stages on the social stratification until 1951 was very much as expected. Large private estates disappeared and with them the political power of the agrarian bourgeoisie. Both the upper and lower sections of the agricultural population shifted towards the middle. Particularly after the limitation of private agricultural holdings to 50 hectares arable land, large peasant holdings became medium-sized peasants while, at the same time, small peasants moved upwards towards the middle, thanks to the process of redistribution. Although the number of small peasant holdings also rose, there was a significant increase in the number as well as the material means of medium-sized peasant holdings (in 1948, 53.8 per cent of all agricultural holdings of between 2 and 50 hectares accounted for 62 per cent of all arable land). Table 8.1 shows that by 1950, after the completion of resettlement and the redistribution of land, the percentage of small and medium-sized peasants had approximately regained the level of 1930 (20.3 per cent compared to 22.3 per cent).

Between 1948 and 1953, small and medium-sized peasants came to form the backbone of the agricultural population. However, the currency reform of 1 June 1953 undermined their financial basis, while the radical policy of collectivisation — which was heralded by the resolution of the IXth Party Congress of the KSČ in 1949 on the 'Transition of the Village to Socialism' — practically eliminated private property among this segment of the agricultural population. A certain number of these formerly independent peasants were absorbed by the agricultural co-operatives (see Table 8.1) while the rest left their villages within the framework of the general exodus from the countryside — a movement which counted over 1 million people in the 20 years between 1948 and 1968, that is, 46 per cent of the population employed in agriculture in 1948 (see Table 7.1). By 1960 the share of the socialist sector in arable land had jumped to 90.9 per cent from 10 per cent in 1948 and, by 1970, had reached 93.1 per cent.

In the 25 years from 1945 to 1970, the Czechoslovak agricultural population displayed an exceptional degree of social mobility which, step by step, reflected the changes taking place in the social relations of agricultural production.

As in the pre-Munich republic, the largest social group in post-war Czechoslovakia was composed of workers and their families. However, the internal structure of the group and its role in society changed beyond recognition. Above all, the political significance of its parties — the Czech SDP and the KSČ — and their trade unions increased dramatically. Furthermore by 1948 the labour movement had been unified through the amalgamation of the Czech SPD with the KSČ, as well as through the centralisation of the formerly fragmented trade unions in the Revolutionary Trade Union movement (Revoluční odborové hnutí — ROH). After February 1948, in line with Marxist theory, official government policy elevated the working class into the leading driving force of the new socialist order. Also in line with Marxist theory, the KSČ was considered to be the vanguard of the working-class movement. It became the foundation stone of the socio-economic transformation of the Czechoslovak economy into a centrally directed and administrated planned economy based on heavy industry.

Although, with an average of 57 per cent during the period from 1930 to 1969 (see Table 8.1), the percentage of workers in the overall social structure of the Czechoslovak population remained basically unchanged, their number grew constantly. In general, the number of female workers increased faster than that of male workers (see p. 99). In terms of branches of industry, the producer-goods industries and the building trade registered the greatest influx of workers because these industries accounted for almost the entire growth of employment between 1948 and 1968 (see Table 7.1), whereas the number of workers declined from the consumer goods industries. This was a reflection of the 'iron concept' on which the planned economy of the 1950s and 1960s was based (see p. 138).

With respect to the regional distribution of industrial workers, their numbers grew in both absolute and relative terms faster in Slovakia than in Czechoslovakia as a whole. Measured according to the number of industrial workers per 1,000 inhabitants, in 1937 there were 103 in Czechoslovakia and 30 in Slovakia; in 1946 the figures were 98 in Czechoslovakia and 41 in Slovakia; by 1961 they had climbed to 170 and 102, until, in 1970, they had reached 188 and 138 respectively.

As these figures show, the apparently static proportion of workers and their families — which constantly accounted for more than half of the total population — conceal a high degree of social mobility: not only in regard to the increase in the number of women in the working population or the movement of workers between different branches of industry and regions, but also in respect of the movement between social levels. The working class swallowed up whole social groups, primarily from the petty bourgeoisie and the agricultural population, as discussed above. Parallel to this influx there was a constant flow of workers moving upwards into intermediate and higher levels of management in the nationalised industries, into the executive organs of the centralised agricultural co-operatives, as well as into the expanding state, security and party apparatuses. Consequently, in the course of the expansion of the centrally administered economy and society, the social group comprising white-collar workers doubled in size between 1950 and 1969 and, in comparison with 1930 (see Table 8.1), actually registered a fourfold increase in numbers. The main criteria for the selection of these white-collar workers, who were recruited from the working class, were reliability and loyalty to the Communist Party and its regime.

At the same time as this major increase in the number of white-collar workers in the structure of post-war society, there was also a remarkable change in their social position. In complete distinction to the pre-Munich republic, the income policy of the post-war government reduced the social gap between industrial workers and white-collar workers. Through a policy of faster wage increases for the lowest paid unskilled workers and slower increases for skilled workers, the government actually succeeded in significantly accelerating a process which had its roots in the 1930s, that is, the trend towards reduced differentials between skilled and white-collar workers. In 1946 the average salary of white-collar workers was 45 per cent higher than the average wage of industrial workers. By 1948 this difference had been reduced to 24.5 per cent.

This was the beginning of a levelling process which encompassed the entire society and which reached its peak between 1951 and 1954. On a symbolic plane, the difference between wages and salaries was officially abolished in the wake of the 1953 currency reform, with all employees drawing their remuneration twice monthly thereafter. By 1955, the average income of white-collar workers had fallen to a level some 14.9 per cent below that of industrial workers. Furthermore, the difference between the traditionally high income of technicians and scientists compared with that of industrial workers had fallen from 65.4 per cent in 1948 to 26.2 per cent in 1955. A statistical picture of the income structure in the socialist sector of the Czechoslovak economy was published in 1959. According to these figures, only 8 per cent of the working population was in receipt of the lowest monthly incomes of up to kčs 800 and only 3 per cent earned more than kčs 2,500, whereas the largest group received between kčs 1,000 and kčs 1,600. These statistics do not include the co-operative peasants who would have boosted the numbers of the lowest income group with average incomes some 30 per cent less than those of industrial workers. Despite the fact that there was a reduction in the differences between the incomes of industrial and agricultural workers — in 1960, it had dropped to 22 per cent — the earnings on the collective farms lagged significantly behind the wages paid in the nationalised industries.

Under the pressure of ever increasing targets set by the central planning authorities, a completely new production-oriented system of values came into being which, within the framework of a general levelling of incomes, was of particular benefit to workers in the mining, heavy, armament and building industries. At the same time, the distinctions between skilled, semi-skilled and unskilled workers, as well as those between qualified workers and university graduates, were blurred. Only in the case of the difference between the incomes of men and women was there hardly any change: although equality had been granted by law, women generally held positions in the lower wage categories. The endeavours of economic reformers in the late 1960s to improve efficiency of the economy through differentiated wage scales did not result in any significant changes in the income structure.

NON-CAPITALIST STRATIFICATION OF SOCIETY

When the census took place in 1961, the process of structural change in the society of Czechoslovakia had been completed with the new social fabric bearing little resemblance to that of the pre-Munich republic (see Table 8.1). As a result of the complete elimination of private business, with the exception of the fees of a small group of artists and authors, the sole legal source of income in Czechoslovakia consisted of wage labour. In the place of the capitalist class society, a less complicated social stratification came into being and was anchored in the new constitution of the Czechoslovak Republic of 11 July 1960, which declared Czechoslovakia to be a socialist state in which Czechs and Slovaks have equal rights. It was laid down that this state was based 'on the firm alliance of workers, peasants and the intelligentsia . . . led by the working class'. According to this official interpretation of events, the socio-economic changes that had been forced through since 1945 resulted in the elimination of the antagonistic capitalist class society — which was characterised by a division into the bourgeoisie and the proletariat — and its replacement with a non-antagonistic social stratification of workers, co-operative peasants and the working intelligentsia.

In the mid-1960s, this formulation was subjected to a thorough sociological investigation by a research team led by Pavel Machonin. The results of this work not only represent a valuable historical document but they also permit a deeper understanding of the new social stratification. The following conclusions are based on this research project.

Without doubt, by 1967, Czechoslovakia had accomplished the most effective process of social levelling of all planned economies in Central and South-east Europe, including the Soviet Union. In conjunction with the levelling of incomes, there was a similar development in the structure of family expenditures covering all social groups. This was influenced by the fact that, since 1955, the costs of personal consumption per inhabitant had been rising faster than real wages (see Table 9.1). As a result of the general rent protection, expenditures on rent remained almost unchanged at a low level, as did services because this sector stagnated. A differentiated picture is only to be found in the expenditures on culture, entertainment and holidays, whereby the families of white-collar workers tended to spend somewhat more — but not very much more — than industrial workers or peasants. In general, there was no great difference in the life-styles of the individual social groups. However, there were significant differences between the sexes. Despite almost full employment among women, they spent approximately one-third less time than men in the pursuit of cultural activities but two and a half times as much time working in the household and on the fields, not to mention 20–30 per cent more time looking after children. In view of the great load borne by women, it is evident that they suffered a relative worsening of their social position between 1948 and 1965. However, this does not alter the general conclusion of the above-mentioned sociological research project that Czechoslovakia's society became significantly more egalitarian due, above all, to the levelling of incomes and the equal rights legislation.

However, the situation changes when we come to look at developments in the political sphere and see how the structure of power has changed since 1948 when the capitalist hierarchy was displaced by a non-capitalist hierarchy. At the top of the new hierarchy was a powerful party, state, security and military apparatus. In the economy, society was divided into two main groups: one of which (an estimated 650,000 to 700,000 people) directed the means of production. Of this group, a much smaller group of approximately 200,000 exercised effective control over the means of production and were responsible for selecting the goods to be produced and determining the distribution of the national income. However, the key decisions in this hierarchy were the preserve of relatively few top planners and, in the last instance, the leaders of the Communist Party — the Politburo. The other group comprising the overwhelming majority of Czechoslovak society had the task in the production process of applying its labour to realise the targets of the planners. In the course of the planning periods since 1948, this became the sole leading function of the workers, whose trade unions — as the 'lever of the KSČ' — were responsible for ensuring fulfilment of the plans handed down to them. From the works councils and co-determination of the immediate post-war years, the reality of Czechoslovak socialism dictated that the workers become passive recipients of planning targets, whereby their initiatives and their interest in renewal, improvements and increased efficiency fell off in proportion to their loss of influence.

EDUCATION AND SOCIETY

Besides the socio-political concentration of power, at the same time Czechoslovakia also witnessed the birth of a socio-professional social hierarchy based on the relatively high educational level of the population and the extremely rapid growth of intellectual, scientific and technical training. It was not just that education and schooling retained their traditionally high ranking in Czechoslovak society but also that their social value increased even more. Accordingly, there was a

Figure 8.1: Pupils in comprehensive schools (state schools) 1945–80

in millions

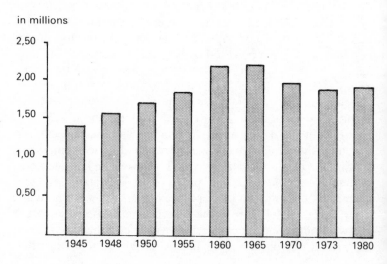

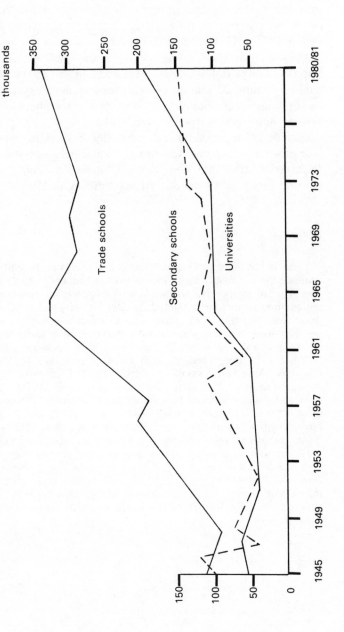

Figure 8.2: Students in higher education in Czechoslovakia, 1945–80/81

dramatic leap in the number of students attending secondary and grammar schools, technical colleges, polytechnics and universities (see Figures 8.1 and 8.2). In proportion to the total employed population, the number of students rose from 8.6 per cent in 1955 to 17.4 per cent in 1966. Nevertheless, the resulting improvement in the level of education and qualification of the population was not adequately reflected in the leading industrial, agricultural, planning and administrative organisations because far more than 50 per cent of the members of these bodies held positions for which they were not properly qualified. On the other hand, education played an important role in society at large. Accordingly, the intelligentsia was able to exercise a certain degree of influence in economic and cultural life, which gained in strength during the 1960s.

Notes

1. Socialisation of private handicrafts and trades in the early 1950s changed the position of this social strata fundamentally. Only a small number of formerly privately owned workshops was integrated into the nationalised sector; an estimated 200,000 formerly independent producers found employment in nationalised industries. Another 100,000 small enterprises joined non-agricultural co-operatives which had been in existence long before 1948. The People's Co-operative Act of 27 October 1954 integrated all such co-operatives into the planned economy. As a result small production units of no more than five members each — which amounted on the average to 125,000 between 1961 and 1979 — serviced to some extent local needs. However, the most important feature of small production, services and trades was created by the Law on Communal Enterprises of 21 July 1948 by which local authorities (*národní výbory* = National Committees) were entrusted with the organisation, employment and control of communal enterprises. All forms of small enterprises in the ČSSR can be subsumed under the term of *local economy* which employed no more than 6 per cent of all persons economically active in 1979. In this sphere part of the former middle strata of society was absorbed (cf. Table 8.1).

9

The Economy and the State

In this chapter, we shall examine developments in the Czechoslovak planned economy in the years from 1945 to 1980. Above
all, the first four five-year plans covering the years between
1948 and 1970 represent a time-span roughly comparable with
that of the pre-Munich republic. This period also covers the
economic reforms of the second half of the 1960s and their
precipitate dismantling consequent on the Soviet-led invasion
by the Warsaw Pact countries in August 1968. In the following
ten years of so-called normalisation between 1970 and 1980, a
further two five-year plans (the fifth and sixth) were passed.
These plans will be included in the evaluation of post-reform
economic developments in Czechoslovakia.

The five-year plans were preceded by a short phase of
reconstruction which went ahead significantly faster in the wake
of the Second World War than after the First. The recovery of
the economy consisted, in the first place, of the initial steps
taken in 1945–6 to relieve the disastrous consequences of the
war and, in the second place, of the two-year plan of 1947 and
1948 which, on the one hand, basically restored the economic
level of 1937 and, on the other, laid the foundations for the
nationalisation of the means of production and the planned
economy.

The war left deep marks in the society (see p. 83) and
economy of Czechoslovakia. Although the territory of the
nation, with the exception of East Slovakia, was not damaged
to the same extent as other areas of Central and South-east
Europe, the cumulative impact of the systematic and increasingly thorough process of exploitation conducted by National
Socialist Germany during six years of occupation, as well as the

destruction wrought by the battles in the closing phase of the war, can only be described as severe. Official and semi-official estimates of the damage amount to between 350 and 430 milliard Czechoslovak crowns, a figure that approximates to the total gross national product of Czechoslovakia in the years from 1932 to 1937. In addition, there is the inestimable and irreplaceable loss of 360,000 victims of the National Socialist regime, as well as another 100,000 ex-prisoners who no longer enjoyed good health as a result of the sufferings inflicted on them in the concentration camps. Czechoslovakia received very little in the way of reparations, because no peace treaty was signed with Germany and its allies. Certain sums were made available by the Inter-Allied Reparation Administration. However, until 1948 when payments ceased, Czechoslovakia only received reparation deliveries with a total value of kčs 500 million, that is, 0.14 per cent of the lowest war-damage estimate. For the immediate relief of suffering, the Soviet Army supplied the Czechoslovak population with food and medicaments, after which the relief campaign of the United Nations Relief and Rehabilitation Administration (UNRRA) started to take effect and contributed significantly to the recovery of allied countries in Europe and, thereby, to that of Czechoslovakia (see p. 118).

Before the reborn state of Czechoslovakia could even regain the level of the pre-war economy, enormous hurdles had to be overcome. After the First World War, Czechoslovakia had detached itself from the larger economic unit of Austria–Hungary. After the Second World War, the various parts of the dismembered economy had to be put back together again. Because the pre-Munich republic had basically been divided into five parts, each of which had developed separately since 1939, the distortions brought about as a direct result of the war had been deepened even further: beside the districts returned from Poland and Hungary, it was necessary to reintegrate the border areas annexed by Germany in 1938 (the so-called Sudetenland), as well as the euphemistically named Protectorate of Bohemia and Moravia and the rump state of Slovakia which was fully separated from the rest of the other parts. Accordingly, one of the political priorities of the Košice Programme was the achievement of an east–west economic balance through accelerated industrialisation in Slovakia (see p. 91).

The Second World War resulted in much greater distortions than the First World War. The main reasons for this were that the extreme demands of arms production overstrained and exhausted the capacities of mining and heavy industry, whereas other branches of industry were technically neglected or practically dismantled. For the transition to peacetime production, long-term measures were essential. In the immediate post-war period, however, there was a great shortage of foodstuffs, raw materials and fuels, and industry worked to only around 40 per cent of full capacity. In May 1945 the average monthly production of coal amounted to only 17 per cent compared to 1937. In the field of brown-coal mining, the figure was 34 per cent. However, the production of pig iron and steel reached no more than 10 and 3.5 per cent respectively. This shortage of coal is particularly noticeable in the stocks held by the railway administration. In the pre-war years, the railways had to hold stocks to cover their daily requirements for at least 42 days. In November 1945, however, their reserves had sunk to just three days. Widespread destruction of railway lines and roads had brought traffic to a complete standstill in many areas. Only 50 per cent of the locomotives were still in the country, with the rest being scattered over the whole continent. Nevertheless, these initial difficulties were overcome relatively quickly and by 1947 the road and rail network had actually surpassed the pre-war level.

Although, compared to May 1945, industrial production had increased by 5–10 per cent by the end of 1945, industrial output was still only 50 per cent and agricultural production only 65 per cent of the 1937 level. Nevertheless, the recovery of the Czechoslovak economy — especially its industrial production — progressed faster than in 1918 and even faster than some comparable West European countries such as France and Belgium. By 1946 production had reached approximately 80 per cent of the pre-war level despite the simultaneous expulsion of the German part of the population. However, agriculture lagged behind the standards set before the war.

Although the structural changes in the economy as a result of the dictates of the German war economy had an extremely negative impact on the post-war economy of Czechoslovakia, the Košice government employed certain instruments of the centralised war economy to overcome the post-war confusion and supply shortages. As in many other European countries, there was a continuation of rationing of vital products, the control of raw materials and fuels, as well as the compulsory sale of agricultural produce. Further elements of the centralised economy were also retained, including the control of prices, wages and the labour market, foreign currency controls, a centralised credit system and foreign trade restrictions. Despite the fact that much of this was an inevitable consequence of the post-war difficulties, a high degree of state intervention was fully in line with the programme of the National Front government, in which the demands of the Communist Party for a 'specific Czechoslovak way to socialism' had a decisive role to play. At this time, the best part of small and medium-sized industrial companies, the bulk of the building trade and almost the entire agricultural sector were still in private hands. However, for Czechoslovakia, the return to peace by no means meant a full return to the market economy of the pre-Munich republic.

Particular problems were caused by the financial situation of the country, as the reborn state not only inherited a devalued currency but also a system of finances in complete disarray. As was the case after the First World War, the government pushed through a far-reaching currency reform (see p. 102) and, finally, set the exchange rate at kčs 50 to US$1. This made it possible for Czechoslovakia to join the International Monetary Fund and provided a basis for its exports. With the passage of time, however, it was only possible to stick to this exchange rate with difficulty and problems were experienced with the budget and the balance of payments.

In the first phase of the process of financial reconstruction, important assistance was rendered to the state finances by UNRRA. During 1946 when the UNRRA aid was at its peak, deliveries of goods amounted to 5 per cent of the Czechoslovak gross national product and 36 per cent of total imports. Because these goods were free of charge but nevertheless could be sold on the domestic market, they contributed to budgetary equilibrium and a more favourable balance of trade. By the end of 1949, Czechoslovakia had received UNRRA goods totalling some kčs 15.5 billion (US$310 million). These supplies covered 28 per cent of the government's expenditures on public health, social services, as well as repatriation and reconstruction costs. In distinction to other recipient countries, however, the UNRRA assistance to Czechoslovakia was not continued with loans for the reconstruction.

Although the USA and Great Britain provided trade credits for Czechoslovakia between 1945 and 1947, they remained largely unused after the possibility of further credit was broken off in June 1947. Consequently, after Czechoslovakia's rejection of the Marshall Plan, the balance of payments moved into deficit and there was a sharp drop in the foreign currency reserves held by the Czechoslovak National Bank. Accordingly, there could be no question of foreign capital playing a leading role in the reconstruction of the economy. The bulk of the capital needed was obtained through the nationalisation of private property — domestic industry and banks — which took place in three waves between 1945 and 1948 (see p. 102). Because foreign holdings were also affected and the compensation negotiations were long and complicated, it became extremely difficult for Czechoslovakia to obtain any credit in the West.

According to contemporary opinion, Czechoslovakia was regarded as 'an island of economic stability' between May 1945 and February 1948. Thanks to its advanced industrial structure and export-oriented economy, it held a special position among the countries of Central and South-east Europe. With the elimination of Germany as a competitor, Czechoslovakia took on an even more important role as an exporter of industrial goods for the extremely deprived East European market. However, the great demand from the West European countries, as well as the domestic market, also had a positive impact on Czechoslovak reconstruction. Although the country's production capacity was restored relatively quickly, it took somewhat longer for exports to pick up. In general, the growth potential of the Czechoslovak economy was the greatest of all Central and South-east European countries. The central factor influencing its specific situation was that the planned economy was introduced into a relatively highly industrialised democracy which, within the framework of the international division of labour, had necessarily been closely linked with the world market since its formation as an independent state. Czechoslovakia's strengths lay in the production of industrial goods. Its weaknesses were to be found in raw material resources. Thus, while retaining the specific features of the Czechoslovak economy, it was objectively possible to employ previously untried methods of planned economic growth differing from those of the Soviet model. Developed on the basis of the prevailing economic situation, the two-year plan (1947 and 1948) was based in many respects on the market mechanism which was to be directed in accordance with the statutory framework created by the government in 1946. This legislation contained elements of an economic democracy which, at grass-roots industrial level, was to be exercised through co-determination in the form of works councils and trade unions and, in the agricultural sector, through peasants' commissions and co-operatives.

THE TWO-YEAR PLAN

The main objective of the two-year plan was to increase the living standards of the Czechoslovak population. If we take 1937 as the base year, the authorities succeeded in this, particularly in terms of national income *per capita* which, as a result of expulsion of almost 2 million inhabitants of German descent, rose relatively more than the figures of gross national product (1937 = 100: GNP in 1948 = 97; national income per capita in 1948 = 113). Of all Central and South-east European countries, only Czechoslovakia succeeded in regaining the pre-war standard of living within three years. Although the aim of a continuously increasing standard of living was theoretically retained in the subsequent five-year plans, it had to give way to the demands of the Stalinist planning concept of the KSČ leadership, which was formulated as the construction of socialism and the attainment of the greatest possible independence from the capitalist states.

In principle, the two-year plan represented the National Front government's programme of renewal and reconstruction which, as mentioned above (see p. 91), was based on a policy of democratic consensus. By the end of 1948, the economic level of 1937 was to have been regained, whereas industrial production was to have been increased by 10 per cent. The favoured position of the industrial sector was reflected in the distribution of capital investments: of the total amount allocated in the plan (kčs 69.88 milliard), 57 per cent was earmarked for the building industry and 43 per cent for the industrial sector. Almost one-third of the total sum to be invested was consciously aimed at accelerating industrialisation in Slovakia, where a rapid catching-up process began. However, the planners' targets were only fulfilled to the tune of 64 per cent because, above all, the building sector was unable to meet the demands of the two-year plan and finished 1948 33 per cent short of expectations. As did the agricultural sector which only reached 80 per cent of the 1937 production level due to insufficient investments and the migration of young workers to the urban areas, as well as the catastrophic drought during the summer of 1947. Furthermore, the international situation, as well as domestic political tensions, began to have a negative effect on the development of the Czechoslovak economy (see p. 103). Nevertheless, despite these shortcomings, the aims of the two-year plan were by and large fulfilled in terms of overall economic indices: especially with respect to national income, transportation and industrial production which, by the end of 1948, exceeded the pre-war level by some 10 per cent. At the end of this period of reconstruction, Czechoslovakia was the sole Central and South-east state to have emulated the West European countries and, basically, to have regained the pre-war standard.

THE MAIN DIRECTIONS OF OVERALL ECONOMIC DEVELOPMENT

The communist ascension to power in 1948 meant a breach with the planning concept of increasing economic democracy. Whereas the two-year plan still permitted market signals to play a role in economic processes, the market mechanism was completely eliminated in the course of the first five-year plan and replaced by central administrative economic planning. This decisive process is discussed in detail in Chapter 10.

Seen from this point of view, it is reasonable if, in Table 9.1, 1948 is taken as the base year (100) for the quantitative estimates of the main overall indicators of economic growth in the period 1948–1970/80, a period that is characterised by the successive five-year plans. In addition to this, numerous official statistical publications of the Organisation for Economic Co-operation and Development (OECD) take 1948 as their base year. This permits economic comparisons to be made both with the pre-Munich republic, as well as in parallel with similarly structured capitalist economies.

At the outset, it should be noted that the data in Table 9.1

Table 9.1: Indicators of economic growth in Czechoslovakia, 1948–80

Indicators	A Development in indices (1948 = 100)						
	1953	1955	1960	1965	1970	1975	1980
National income[1]	156	178	251	277	386	510	611
Per capita national income	150	168	227	241	332	425	492
Industrial production	193	224	372	480	665	921	1,156
of this: producer goods A	219	249	434	576	808	1,134	1,444
Consumer goods B	166	197	307	378	516	697	838
Agricultural production	116	126	136	132	168		
Gross fixed investment	237	249	465	513	725	1,077	1,277
in the productive sector	231	235	500	566	747	1,129	1,402
in the non-productive sector	249	281	392	403	683	971	1,024
Employment	102	107	109	117	127	134	139
of this in industry	113	118	138	151	161	188	195
in agriculture	83	86	66	56	53	46	44
in the non-productive sector	116	126	144	186	220	239	257
Export turnover	131	155	261	374	522	943	1,567
Social productivity	155	170	246	271	348	436	496
Average wage[3] (workers in the socialist sector)	133	146	166	181	235	279	321
Personal consumption per inhabitant	115	138	181	202	260	319	335

Notes: [1] Comecon concept — created national income.

[2] Absolute figures at the last year of each planning period (thousands): 5,545 in 1948; 5,683 in 1953; 5,956 in 1955; 6,063 in 1960; 6,871 in 1970; 7,060 in 1975.

[3] Without peasants from co-operatives.

[4] Interim period.

[5] F. Levcik, *Czechoslovakia*, pp. 380, 412.

[6] 1950–53.

[7] Employment in industry and agriculture.

B Rate of growth in % — annual averages of planning periods

1948–53	1953–55[4]	1955–60	1960–65	1965–70	1971–75[5]	1976–80
9.3	7.1	7.1	2.0	6.9	5.7	3.7
8.6	5.5	6.0	1.4	7.5	5.6	3.1
14.1	7.8	10.7	5.3	6.7	6.7	5.0
18.5[6]	6.7	11.7	5.8	7.2	7.1	6.1
8.2[6]	9.0	9.3	4.3	7.9	5.7	2.6
3.0	4.2	1.6	−0.6	4.8	2.6	5.4
19.1	2.7	13.3	2.4	7.2	8.2	3.5
15.3	0.8	16.4	2.9	5.8	8.6	4.5
20.0	6.3	7.1	4.1	11.3	7.3	1.1
0.4	2.4	0.4	1.3	1.7	2.8	2.9[2]
0.1	2.1	−0.0	0.5	1.2	1.5	1.3[7]
—	—	2.8	5.8	3.6	7.2	8.5
5.5	9.2	10.9	7.4	6.9	12.6	10.7
9.2	4.7	7.7	2.0	5.2	—	—
5.9	4.6	2.6	1.8	5.4	3.4	1.2
3.5	11.1	6.4	3.0	5.4	4.8	2.6

Sources: V. Průcha et al., Hospodářské dějiny Československa v 19. a 20. století (Prague, 1974); Statistická ročenka ČSSR, relevant years; 25 let Československa 1945–70, (Prague, 1970); F. Levcik, Czechoslovakia: economic performance in post-reform period and prospects for the 1980s in East European assessment, Part I — Country Studies, 1980 (Washington, 1981); 30 let ČSSR Dlouhodobé časové řady (30 years ČSSR long series) (Prague, 1975); WIFO, Volkswirtschaftliche Datenbank, Wien.

detailing the course of economic development in Czecho-slovakia from 1948 to 1970/80 is based on official statistics from Czechoslovakia and from the Vienna Institute for International Economic Comparisons. In a number of studies (see Biblio-graphy), the criteria and the methods of calculation employed in official publications of the Federální statistický úřad (Federal Statistical Office) in Prague have been called into question. This applies particularly to figures of national income calculated in accordance with the concept of the countries of the Council for Mutual Economic Assistance (CMEA or Comecon). However, despite the fact that the statistics of national income calculated by a number of authors in accordance with Western concepts are not only different from the Czechoslovak results but also from each other, a general trend can nevertheless be discerned. Accord-ingly, the Czechoslovak statistics can be used to illustrate the dynamic process of economic growth, provided it is not forgotten that statistics of national income calculated in accordance with the Comecon concept correspond with the Western interpretation of net material product (NMP) and represent the total net value of all material products and the associated services. According to this interpretation, the social product and, thus, national income is based exclusively on activities in the productive branches of the economy listed in Table 7.1. From this table, it can be seen that, between 1948 and 1968, the number of people employed in the unproductive sector rose from 12 per cent to over 20 per cent of the total labour force and, as the indicators in Table 9.1 show, continued to grow thereafter. According to the Comecon concept, this sector does not contribute to national wealth because it is not directly linked with material production. However, it is included in the Western national income statistics. In order to be able to compare the production, distribution and utilisation of the post-war national income with the pre-Munich republic, J. Krejčí's conversions, in which the Comecon figures have been adapted to the Western basis, have been incorporated in Tables 3.2 and 3.3.

Compared with the inter-war years, there was a significant increase in the rate of overall economic growth in Czecho-slovakia during the years from 1948 to 1980 (see Table 9.1). National income increased almost fourfold by 1970 and sixfold by 1980. Industrial production expanded by over six and a half times by 1970 and reached 1,156 index points in the subsequent decade (1948 = 100). With a 27 per cent increase in the size of the labour force between 1948 and 1980, there was an increase in the index of social productivity (that is, the relationship of national income to the number of people in gainful employment in the productive sector). Although this did not take place at the same speed as the national income (611 points in 1980), the index nevertheless rose to 496 points in 1980. Furthermore, the value of Czechoslovak exports increased by a factor of over five. Hence, when we consider aggregate rates of growth in this period, the economic performance of Czechoslovakia is certainly comparable with that of similarly structured Western industrial nations.

Far less successful, on the other hand, was the performance of the agriculture sector, both in comparison with the pre-Munich republic, as well as with the capitalist countries, with the 1937 level not being reached until some 20 years later. With an increase of just under two and a half times, the figures for average wages also rose significantly less rapidly than other indicators of economic development in Czechoslovakia. Accordingly, the volume of personal consumption, which climbed by a factor of slightly more than two and a half, kept more or less pace with wage developments. According to calculations of the real wages of workers and white-collar workers, their incomes doubled in the period between 1937 and 1970 while the cost of living index rose less, reaching only 122 index points. However, compared with comparable capitalist economies in Western Europe, growth rates of wages, consumption and services in Czechoslovakia stagnated at a level far below the average.

In historical perspective, the process of structural change which had started in the pre-Munich republic (see p. 34) was continued at a faster, planned rate. It was completed through a fundamental restructuring of the economy in mutual dependence on the changes in social stratification mentioned above (see p. 102f.). Table 3.2 shows the shifts in the national product according to economic sectors. These shifts are reflected in the distribution (Table 3.3) and utilisation of national income (Table 9.2). Whereas structural change according to sectors displays similar characteristics to that taking place in the Western industrial countries, particularly in the reduction in the primary sector, it differs in the relationship of growth between the secondary and tertiary sectors (according to the Comecon

Table 9.2: Utilisation of the gross national product, 1930–77 (in %)

	ČSR		ČSSR		
	1930	1937	1948	1967	1977
Private consumption	70.3	67.9	65.1	50.9	50.0
Public consumption	11.3	16.2	17.0	18.2	22.2
Gross capital investment	17.8	17.1	15.1	23.8	26.3
'Market buffer' (inventories and balances of goods and services)[1]	0.6	-1.2	2.8	7.1[2]	1.5[2]
Total	100.0	100.0	100.0	100.0	100.0

Notes: [1] Due to the separation from the world market inventories increased as a necessary 'Market buffer' which slowed down economic growth.

[2] Includes statistically published losses.

Sources: J. Krejčí, 'Volkseinkommenvergleich', p. 17; and *National Income and Outlay*, p. 23.

concept, the relationship of sector A — the productive sector — to sector B — the non-productive sector — changed from 1.15:1 in 1950 to 2.10:1 in 1980). The shift in emphasis to the production of investment goods is demonstrated by the growth of the industrial and building sectors from 44.7 per cent in 1930 to 58.9 per cent in 1977 in contrast to the insignificant increase in the service sector and the distinct lag in agricultural production (see Table 3.2).

Despite the fact that the general trend shows common characteristics, even more striking deviations from the process of structural change in the capitalist states appear as a result of an analysis of the changes in the structure of the various branches of industry. Table 9.3 is a comparison of 1958 and 1966 with 1937 (100) in which — apart from the increase in chemical production which equates with the Western rates of growth — the mechanical engineering sector makes the most dramatic leap to 1,230 index points and thereby exhibits the fastest rate of growth of this branch of the economy in comparison with the advanced industrial nations. Growth rates approaching this level were also recorded in the energy sector (reaching 1,068 index points in 1966), while the metallurgical industry kept pace with the aggregate rate of industrial growth and with the fast rates of development in other industrial coun-

Table 9.3: Changes in the structure of Czechoslovak industrial production, 1937–66

Branch of industry	1948	1958	1966	1937	1948	1958	1966
		(1937 = 100)			(in %)		
Total industry	108	326	559	100	100	100	100
Fuels	138	301	442	7.8	11.0	8.4	7.4
Energy	198	551	1,068	1.6	2.8	2.7	3.2
Metallurgy	111	313	551	9.4	13.3	13.2	13.9
Engineering[1]	123	611	1,230	16.6	13.0	22.7	27.3
Chemical industry	164	664	1,759	2.6	2.5	3.6	5.7
Consumer goods industry	100	227	334	30.7	25.8	20.6	18.1
Food industry	89	209	284	28.1	28.6	23.7	19.2

Note: [1] All metalworking branches of industry.
Source: *50 let hospodářský a společenský vývoj Československa* (50 years of economic and social development of Czechoslovakia), p. 44.

tries, for example, Czechoslovak steel production increased by two and a half times in the same period as steel production in Italy and Japan rose by a factor of more than three and a half. In contrast to this relatively good performance, the consumer goods and food processing industries recorded far below average growth rates with 334 and 284 index points respectively (compare the change in percentage shares of the individual branches in total industrial production shown in Table 9.3).

In general, as a feature of economic growth during the post-war years, the distribution of gross capital investment played a decisive role in the structural changes taking place between both the sectors and the branches of industry. However, there are fundamental differences in the starting points of the Western and the Comecon economic systems which determine the various levels of investment. In the capitalist system investments are basically made in accordance with effective demand, whereas in planned economies investments with a view to growth are determined from the supply side. According to this point of view, the main function of investments is to expand production capacities and, thereby, create the framework for a constant increase in national income which, theoretically, will provide maximum satisfaction of the needs of society. Therefore, in Czechoslovakia, the decision-making process for the distribution of gross capital investments takes place in the administrative system according to primary political directives from the central planning body where the requests for investment resources from companies and other economic, social and cultural institutions come together. Because Czechoslovakia is highly industrialised but not self-sufficient in terms of energy and raw materials, the investment policies have far-reaching effects on the economic life of the country, which we will deal with in more detail in Chapter 10. In order to be able to make an historical analysis of the problems which thereby arose for Czechoslovakia, it is necessary to examine the basic trends of the investment movement and their reciprocal influence on the development of other significant economic indicators.

Between 1948 and 1975, gross capital investments rose by a factor of over ten and by 1980 reached 1,277 index points. Since the 1950s, the productive branches of industry had regularly

Table 9.4: Distributive shares of gross capital investment in the Czechoslovak economy, 1948–75 (in %)

Sector	1948–55[1]	1956–60[1]	1961–65[2]	1966–75[2]
Productive sector	70.0	73.0	74.4	71.8
Industry	42.3	40.3	42.9	37.7
Building	2.1	3.0	2.6	3.8
Agriculture and forestry	10.4	16.3	15.0	11.6
Transport and communication	12.9	10.1	10.4	11.7
Trade	1.2	2.1	2.0	3.2
Others	1.1	1.2	1.5	3.8
Unproductive sector	30.0	27.0	25.6	28.2
Science and research	0.6	0.9	1.0	1.3
Housing	18.0	15.7	15.2	15.7
Health and social security	2.0	1.4	1.5	1.6
Schools, culture and sport	3.0	4.1	4.1	4.8
Communal services and administration	6.4	4.9	3.8	4.8
Total	100.0	100.0	100.0	100.0

Notes: [1] In 1964 prices.
        [2] In 1967 prices.
Source: F.L. Altmann and J. Sláma, *Strukturentwicklung der tschechoslowakischen Wirtschaft und ihre Rüchwirkung auf den Aussenhandel* (Osteuropa-Institut, Munich, December 1979), p. 5 (calculated from *Statistická ročenka* 1966, 1972, 1976).

128

received preferential treatment so that by 1980 the index of investments in the productive sector had climbed to 1,402, whereas the figure in the unproductive sector had only reached 1,024 (see Table 9.1). Developments in the individual branches of industry is shown in Table 9.4 for the years 1948 to 1975. Taken as a whole, the continuous upwards trend in investments moved in line with the increase in employment and with the growing level of industrial output (see Table 9.1). Once again, the priority accorded to industrial production is very noticeable. On average, it accounted for 60 per cent of total investments. In percentage terms, agricultural investments rose from 1948 to 1960 and 1965, that is, from 10.4 per cent to 16.3 per cent and 15 per cent but then fell in the subsequent decade to 11.6 per cent. In the unproductive sphere, the share of gross capital investments fell over the same period of time from 30 per cent to 28.2 per cent. Within this framework, however, expenditures on scientific activities and research, as well as schools, culture and sport, increased to a relatively large extent from 0.6 per cent to 1.3 per cent and from 3 per cent to 4.8 per cent (see Table 9.4).

The main indicators for the course of growth are the priorities in the distribution of gross capital investments in the various branches of industry. They are shown in Table 9.5 for the period 1951 to 1977. Long statistical series point to changes in the industrial structure: whereas mechanical engineering accounted for the largest proportion (on average approx. 18 per cent) — incidentally, maintaining its predominant position from the time of the pre-Munich republic — the fuel and metallurgical industries show an above average share until the mid-1960s. From the middle of the 1960s until the 1970s, there was a certain change in the priorities of the planners because, in comparison with the years from 1949 to 1965, investments in the fuel and metallurgical industries begin to fall off in favour of the consumer-goods industries. In this period, investment activity in the consumer-goods industries approached the average level, although the export-oriented industries, such as glass, porcelain and ceramics, received above-average allocations. Reflected in this are the incomplete economic and financial reforms of the later 1960s which, however, made no major changes in the basic trend of economic growth in Czechoslovakia.

Of all indicators that illuminate the basic trends of Czechoslovak economic growth, the greatest relative increases are

129

Table 9.5: Distributive shares of gross capital investment in Czechoslovak industry, 1951–77 (in %)

Branches of industry	1951–55	1956–60	1961–65	1966–70	1971–75	1976–77
Fuels and energy	26.8	34.2	26.9	21.4	22.8	24.6
Fuels	12.4	18.7	14.5	10.2	9.9	9.6
Energy	14.4	15.5	12.4	11.2	12.9	15.0
Raw material processing						
Industries	34.3	29.4	33.6	29.7	26.4	26.0
Metallurgy	19.9	15.5	17.4	10.9	7.9	9.1
Chemicals	10.1	7.4	11.2	12.6	11.8	11.7
Building materials	4.3	6.5	5.0	6.2	6.7	5.2
Commodity production	27.2	24.8	27.0	31.7	32.9	33.2
Engineering	17.4	16.0	17.7	18.0	18.6	21.0
Consumer goods industry	8.8	8.8	9.3	13.7	14.3	12.2
Food and other industries	12.7	11.6	12.5	17.2	17.9	16.2
Food industry	4.7	4.5	5.1	7.1	7.4	7.4
Others	8.0	7.1	7.4	10.1	10.5	8.8
Total investment in industry	100.0	100.0	100.0	100.0	100.0	100.0

Source: F.L. Altmann and J. Sláma, p. 17 (calculated from *Statistická ročenka*, 1974, p. 209; 1978; p. 209).

recorded by gross capital investments in the productive sector and the figures for the output of producer goods (see Table 9.1). This confirms that the constant expansion of investments and the increase in accumulation, especially in the growth of fixed assets (see indicators in Table 9.1), retained a central position in the priorities of the planned economy during the entire period under discussion here. For an analysis of the basic trends of economic growth in Czechoslovakia between 1948 and 1980, this perception is of fundamental importance.

Taking the general economic data, the dynamics of Czechoslovak development after 1948 are shown by the growth rates. Whereas the aggregate indicators rise constantly, the growth rates fluctuate in a wave-like movement but with a declining tendency over the long run (see Table 9.1). Thanks to the input of great factor reserves, the growth rate increased up until the middle of the 1950s. However, in subsequent years, the dynamics of growth slowed continuously and, between 1962 and 1964, showed negative rates of growth in national income and in gross output of industry and agriculture.

In the capitalist economies, periodic crises are a familiar feature of the trade cycle. Although the overall statistical series of Czechoslovakia's centrally controlled economy do not match the cyclical fluctuations of the Western economies, they nevertheless reveal high and low phases occurring regularly between 1948 and 1980. Peaks can be seen in the annual rates of growth of gross capital investment, the output of the producer goods industries, as well as national income created and used, in 1950–52, 1958–9, 1965–6 and 1975–6. Troughs, corresponding with periodic cycles of seven to ten years are evident in 1954, 1963, 1969–70 and 1979–80. Neither peaks nor troughs occur at the same time as the beginning and end phases of the five-year plans.

Simultaneously, there was a cyclical movement linked with the level of investment in the components of accumulation which are composed, first, of the annual growth of capital assets (that is, the increase of fixed assets — also known as the capital stock or basic fund), secondly, of changes in the sum of unfinished investment projects and, thirdly, changes in inventories. A comparison of these series of data shows that increases in investments in the productive sector are followed at two- to three-year intervals by increasing inventories and growing numbers of unfinished investment projects and that, in the case of reductions in investments, there is a movement in the opposite direction; in other words, inventories and the number of unfinished projects fall when larger quantities of completed plant and equipment are taken into operation, as a rule after long construction times. The comparison also shows that on average between 1955 and 1980 a third of total accumulation was accounted for by unfinished projects and inventories. This resulted in disproportions and bottlenecks in the supply sector and therefore was a restraining influence on growth rates in production. Shifts within the structure of the utilised national income in the same period illustrate the long-term negative effect of this development on the national income available to the economy (see Table 9.2). For, according to Czechoslovak national income accounting, the accumulation quota is that part of used national income representing the expansion of national resources and, to the greatest possible extent, serves production and consumption, that is, it should serve to satisfy the needs of society through the expansion of production capacities. From a share of 7.4 per cent in 1948, the accumulation quota grew to 20 per cent in 1960 and 25 per cent in 1980. However, due to the constantly disproportionate share of unfinished investment projects and inventories, a significant part of the increase in total useable national income was taken out of economic circulation. In the main, this took place at the cost of personal consumption which, in the 25 years being discussed here, fell by approximately 10 per cent. These reciprocal relationships were also clearly dependent on the general phases of economic growth: the growth of inventories and the number of unfinished projects declined consequent on peaks and increased consequent on troughs in the eight- to nine-year cycles which occurred in the basic trends of Czechoslovak economic development.

As in the Czechoslovak economy, quantitative evidence of cyclical changes in economic growth can also be given for Poland, Hungary and the GDR. These economic cycles were analysed by leading Comecon economists, firstly in Poland, above all by M. Kalecki, O. Lange and W. Brus, then in Czechoslovakia in the 1960s by J. Goldmann, J. Flek and K. Kouba and in Hungary in the 1970s by T. Bauer. For many years, the existence of economic cycles in planned economies was denied by official sources and, until the late 1960s, described by Soviet economists as a fabrication. However, during the various attempts at economic reform — not just in the ČSSR — it became evident that consideration would have to be given to this fact of economic development and that certain aspects of the fluctuations with a simultaneous reduction in the rate of economic growth were linked with the effects of investment policy in planned economies and therefore with the whole question of political directives in a centrally controlled administrative system. From the point of view of economic history, an explanation is only to be found in the economic policy of the Communist Party and the Czechoslovak planning system. And this will be examined in the following chapter.

10

The Centrally Planned Economy

The orientation of post-war economic policy in all countries of Central and South-east Europe was decisively influenced by the presence of the Soviet Army. Czechoslovakia was the only state of the region able to make an immediate start on an effective policy of reconstruction, the basic tenets of which (annulment of the Munich Agreement, alliance with the USSR, resettlement of the Germans) had been agreed with the Allies before the end of the war. Political sympathy in Czechoslovakia was with the USSR as the liberator from the National Socialist oppressors, while the withdrawal of the Soviet troops in November 1945 reinforced this feeling of trust. At the same time, however, the Czechoslovak authorities aimed for friendly relations with the Western Allies.

It was against this background that economic planning took its initial steps with the start of the two-year plan. This was followed by a series of five-year plans, the economic and political framework of which will be discussed in the following sections.

RESTRUCTURING THE ECONOMY TO CONFORM WITH A CENTRALLY ADMINISTERED AND DIRECTED SYSTEM OF PLANNING AND CONTROL (1948–53)

In connection with the diverse range of opinions about economic planning within the pluralist National Front government, there was a struggle to gain control of the reins of power which the communists had won in February 1948. Accordingly, the concept of the KSČ giving priority to a restructuring of

134

production with the emphasis on heavy industry and rapid industrialisation in Slovakia was passed by the Czechoslovak Parliament on 27 October 1948, with the law introducing the first five-year plan. During the initial phase, consideration was still given to the specific way of the Czechoslovak economy. Between 1949 and 1952, however, it came to radical changes which eliminated the market mechanism and banished the expectation that Czechoslovakia's economic relations would develop with the capitalist as well as the socialist world.

By February 1949 all initiatives in the direction of economic democracy — including the pluralistic Central Planning Commission with its economic experts, representatives of all political parties and trade unions — had been suppressed. Despite the fact that it had introduced a workable system of control, the Central Planning Commission was replaced by the State Planning Office holding ministerial rank. As the supreme planning body, it was at the top of a hierarchy with four main levels: immediately subordinate to the State Planning Office were the ministers for the individual branches of industry who, in turn, were in charge of the main administrative bodies. Right at the bottom were the enterprises. This pyramid formed the basis of the centrally administered planned economy and was an imitation of the Soviet system which took no account of the different social and economic conditions existing between the two countries. This mechanical transplantation of the Soviet system took place throughout Eastern Europe, except in Yugoslavia, with the maximisation of economic growth through the greatest possible increase in production becoming the basis for all economic theory and planning.

External events had a decisive impact on the working of the first five-year plan. Determined to a large extent by America's monopoly of nuclear weapons at that time, the Cold War intensified with the imposition of the embargo against the USSR and the Peoples' Democracies of Eastern Europe, with the formation of the North Atlantic Treaty Organisation (NATO) in April 1949, and with the separation of those zones of Germany occupied by the Western Allies from the rest of the country to form the Federal Republic of Germany (FRG) on 23 May 1949. The counter measures in Eastern Europe followed in quick succession after the breach between the Soviet Union and Yugoslavia in June 1948 and, in particular, are marked by the foundation of the Council for Mutual Economic Assistance

(Comecon) in January 1949 and the establishment of the German Democratic Republic (GDR) on 30 May 1949.

As the most advanced Comecon country, Czechoslovak industry was allocated oversized tasks which made it impossible for the country to follow its 'specific way to socialism': on the one hand, Czechoslovakia had to make a major contribution to the industrialisation of the other member countries and, on the other hand, it had to rebuild and significantly expand its armaments production. Carried out hastily under the guidance of Soviet experts, the restructuring considered necessary had a long-term impact on the structure of the economy of the post war republic.

At the beginning of 1949, there was no sympathy in the Comecon for the Czechoslovak proposal to co-ordinate the production plans of the member countries. Instead of a division of labour and integration, autarkic tendencies became dominant and, on the whole, any co-operation was limited to trade relations. Furthermore, Czechoslovakia became the subject of criticism among the Comecon members for not sufficiently cutting back its trade with the West. Consequently, the share of the USSR and the Peoples' Democracies in the foreign trade statistics of Czechoslovakia rose from 39.6 per cent in 1948 to 78.5 per cent in 1953, whereby the export volume of machines, manufacturing plant and tools doubled (from 20.3 per cent to 40.4 per cent). Accordingly, Czechoslovakia became the machine shop of Eastern Europe and because it subordinated its own needs to the demands of industrialisation of the other Comecon states it was unable to solve either the problems caused by high raw material costs — the result of inadequate domestic raw material resources — or its foreign trade problems in relation to the world market.

At the same time, the effort involved in high-pressure armaments production strained the Czechoslovak economy to breaking point. This is an aspect which tends to have been neglected by economic historians to date. The defence policy requirements strained the economy in two directions: in the first place, there was the modernisation of the Czechoslovak armed forces, for example, motorisation of the army, equipping it with tanks and setting up an air force capable of defending the country; secondly, there was the enormous increase in the production of a wide range of armaments and munitions for export. Between 1950 and 1952 alone, there was a fourfold increase in the output of the armaments industry. All told, the exaggerated part played by the Ministry of Defence in the Czechoslovak economy had a crippling effect on the production of peacetime goods; the location of heavy industry was selected on strategic instead of economic considerations; the road and railway network was adapted to military needs and reserves of material and young workers were withdrawn from the production process.

Table 10.1: Increase in targets of first five-year plan, 1948–53 (1948 = 100)

	Original plan	Revised plan	Fulfilment of plan
	1948	1951	1953
National income	148	170	159
Industrial production	157	198	193
Producer goods industry	166	233	213
Consumer goods and food industry	150	173	166
Engineering industry	193	291	323
Chemical industry	162	210	238
Textile industry	168	–	139
Agricultural production	137	153	117

Sources: Vladimír Nachtigal, *Národní důchod Československa* (National income of Czechoslovakia), (Prague, 1969), p. 114; Václav Průcha *et al.*, p. 298.

In February 1951 the Central Committee of the KSČ decided to increase the plan figures of the first five-year plan — which were scheduled to be fulfilled by 1953 — without taking into account the objective possibilities of the Czechoslovak economy (see Table 10.1). While the production plan, that is, for fuel and energy, cement and basic chemical materials, was almost doubled, the planners reckoned with a reduction in the output of the export industries, that is, by a quarter in the case of wool and cotton yarns and by a third in the case of shoes. At the same time, the investment plan was increased by 50 per cent — in the case of heavy industry by no less than 75 per cent. It was only possible to cope with these drastic interventions in the economic structure of the country by taking strict centralised control of the economic processes and applying political pressure.

Although the planned targets were not achieved, industrial production rose by 93 per cent between 1948 and 1953 (by 128 per cent in Slovakia). This corresponds with an overall annual rate of growth of 14 per cent (18 per cent in Slovakia) or 17 per cent in the case of production goods and 10 per cent for consumer goods. National income increased by 56 per cent and the annual rate of growth reached 9.3 per cent. Gross capital investments leaped by 173 per cent. However, agricultural production rose by only 16 per cent (between 1951 and 1953, it actually fell); compared with the target of 53 per cent, *per capita* consumption increased by a mere 15 per cent. In other words, the standard of living lagged significantly behind the level planned. Without doubt, the industrial potential of the ČSR was increased by a remarkable degree. However, it resulted in unbalanced growth characterised by a parallel negligence, not just of the agricultural sector and the consumer goods industries but also of transport and communications, as well as housing and the tertiary sector.

This unparalleled rate of growth between 1949 and 1953 was regarded by the party, government and industry, as well as their bureaucratic apparatuses, as evidence of success. It appeared to confirm the principle of the infallible leadership of the Soviet Union and the Communist Party and to emphasise the possibility of achieving socialism and communism within a very short space of time. However, it was not long before the negative consequences of this policy of maximum instead of optimum growth began to manifest themselves. As the incidence of bottlenecks and failures increased, they were linked with the perfidious activities of 'enemies of the state and spies', the spectre of which played a central role in the 'personality cult' of the time (the peak of Stalinism) and, in the show trials of the 1950s, led to numerous people being sentenced to long terms of imprisonment or death under the slogan, 'the enemy in our own ranks'. Naturally, although this scapegoat policy spread fear and put the population under political pressure, it was unable to reverse the consequences of misdirected planning.

For the agricultural sector, the 'transition of the village to socialism' was announced in 1949, in accordance with the resolution of the IX KSČ Party Congress within the framework of the general 'construction of socialism'. This was immediately followed by a radical and mechanically implemented process of collectivisation which resulted in the loss of valuable experience of the peasants and the progressive co-operatives of Central Europe's most efficient agricultural system. The majority of the new Unified Agricultural Co-operatives (Jednotné zemědělské družstvo — JZD) came under the control of unqualified personnel. However, the destruction of the small and medium-sized agricultural units did not automatically mean that the large co-operative operations could be developed effectively. Above all, this was due to a lack of funds for investments, the bulk of which went into heavy industry. These problems were compounded by the negative consequences of official pricing policy: average prices for farm produce lagged behind retail trade prices and agricultural expenses. There was a lack of incentives to increase production (see Table 10.1). This led to a further long-term fall in the numbers of people interested in working on the land and accelerated the migration of the best and young workers into the industrial sector.

As a result of the priority given to the producer-goods industries, the tertiary sector was left behind as planned (see p. 129) and services only expanded in those areas where they were of benefit to heavy industry. The first five-year plan dealt no less severely with the consumer-goods industries. Investments were cut back to such an extent that demand greatly exceeded supply. Thus, it was necessary to retain rationing, to avoid fanning the developing flames of inflation. However, as these measures proved to be inadequate, the inflation problem was tackled in a more radical fashion with the currency reform of 1 June 1953 (see p. 104): the purchasing power of the population was dramatically curtailed and the planners were able to abolish rationing, as well as significantly increase retail prices. At the same time, the retail trade and small-scale industries were brought under state administration (see p. 104). From this point in time, the price system was fully separated from supply and demand and served mainly as an instrument of central planning, in order, through high prices, to limit the consumption of consumer goods, excepting vital foodstuffs, and, through low prices for producer goods, to pave the way for heavy industry. There was no reduction in the difficulties of satisfying the personal needs of the population because due to the economic imbalances mentioned above the economy developed into a state-controlled sellers' market.

THE CONSEQUENCES OF THE CENTRALLY ADMINISTERED AND DIRECTED SYSTEM OF PLANNING AND CONTROL: BARRIERS TO GROWTH AND ECONOMIC CRISIS (1953–63)

In general, the rate of growth of economic development began to fall. During the period 1953–4, there was a partial drop in the dynamic force of economic growth (see Table 9.1B). Although these negative indications did not remain unidentified in contemporary Czechoslovakia, criticism was not tolerated and within the rigid framework of the centrally administered and directed system there were no effective instruments capable of rapidly correcting planning mistakes. Because cost-benefit analysis had been abandoned, production costs, income, profits and prices could neither form the basis for entrepreneurial decisions nor measure the efficiency of economic units. The market mechanism had been eliminated from the area of production but not from the areas of consumption and the distribution of labour. For the enterprises, it was a matter of indifference: whether their products were finding buyers or simply keeping the warehouse shelves full; whether they were making profits or losses; or whether investments were used rationally. The sole measure of success was the fulfilment of the planned targets which, from the head office to the individual works, were laid down mechanically and in detail, prescribing the actual physical quantities each individual economic unit was to produce. Because fulfilling the plan also determined the distribution of materials and financial resources, enterprises tended to exaggerate and falsify their reports of success, to inflate demands on investment funds, labour and wages funds, as well as unnecessarily to hoard scarce raw materials and hold excessively large stocks. In this way, distorted information influenced the decision-making process right up to the highest levels: in the State Planning Office, in the Central Commission for People's Control and in the Central Committee of the Communist Party.

Officially regarded as the only possible and correct course to take, these economic methods were reinforced by the simultaneous introduction of the Soviet budgetary and taxation system which suspended price relations and separated the domestic market from the world market. The whole financial system was relegated to a mere system of evidence. This can be illustrated with the changed role of the banks which simply became executive organs of official planning policy. Thus the Central Bank became the instrument of the government's monetary and credit policy. It no longer operated a flexible bank rate, minimum reserves or an open market policy in support of the currency and, because the bank rate had become superfluous, the volume of money had to be rigidly laid down and the exchange rate fixed. The Central Bank was only permitted to credit-finance production in accordance with predetermined rates of interest and repayment schedules (investment loans at 6 per cent, working credits at 4 per cent). It also received instructions regarding the amounts and the dates on which it had to collect money from the enterprises and which sums were to be paid out to which companies. In other words, the function of the Central Bank was limited to providing evidence of the state of plan-fulfilment in the individual economic units. Furthermore, there were four types of bank, each with distinctly separate tasks. The Investment Bank existed to settle old transactions (from the pre-planning period) and drifted along in the direction of its dissolution. A network of Savings Banks gathered in private savings which received interest of 1.7 per cent for short-term deposits and 3–5 per cent for long-term deposits. The savings banks were only permitted to grant consumer credits at an interest rate of 3 per cent. These loans were repaid by deductions direct from wages. In addition, there was the Commercial Bank, which was solely responsible for financing domestic foreign-trade organisations on the basis of foreign-trade plans and contracts, and the Trade Bank which only served foreign clients in Czechoslovakia and abroad, as well as Czechoslovak organisations abroad. Other than private savings, the banks were unable to collect large sums of money in their accounts because the relatively low interest rates did not attract capital from enterprises. This often led to ill-considered and unproductive investments or simply to a waste of money by the managements of such enterprises.

Under the conditions of the central planning apparatus created in the course of the first five-year plan, there were hardly any possibilities for deviations from the centrally controlled economic system, and even less for the implementation of an economic reform.

In the field of foreign policy, there was a slow relaxation of tensions after the end of the Korean War in the summer of 1953. Although this practically ended the Cold War in the spring of the following year, East–West relationships soon deteriorated again as a result of the unrest in Poland, the Soviet intervention in Hungary and the Suez crisis.

Domestically, there were few changes in Czechoslovakia, even after the death of Stalin and, immediately thereafter, the death of Gottwald at the beginning of 1953. The reins of power were taken over by Antonın Zápotocký, as President of the Republic, and Antonín Novotný as the Secretary of the Central Committee of the Czechoslovak Communist Party. In 1957, following the death of Zápotocký, these two highest offices were held by Novotný. Both Zápotocký and Novotný ranked among those leaders who had identified themselves with the show trials. Accordingly, they were reluctant to react to the pressure from the party basis to investigate and make reparations for the interventions in political and economic life, as well as diverse miscarriages of justice. Although an Investigation and Rehabilitation Commission was nominated by the Communist Party in 1955, its work proceeded only haltingly and did not begin to accelerate until the 1960s.

In the economy, however, the precipitate process of collectivisation, the falling standard of living and the severe currency reform at the end of the first five-year plan led to increasing political tensions and, consequently, there was a temporary break in the strict pursuit of the planned targets. Between 1953 and 1955, this pressure forced the leaders of the Czechoslovak Communist Party to make some concessions to public consumption and mitigate the collectivisation and investment policy through the insertion of two one-year plans. Nevertheless, the subsequent five-year plans basically followed the line initiated by the first five-year plan. With the exception of the brief but epoch-making reform movement between 1966 and 1968 (see p. 151f.), the priorities of the central planners remained economic growth based on continuous increases in investment, as well as greater output of producer goods and higher and higher defence expenditures. Therefore, these problems repeated themselves in the long run, albeit with varying degrees of severity.

The basic principles of the five-year plans soon ran up against barriers to growth. Although these barriers became evident in all Comecon countries, they were quickly reached in Czechoslovakia because it was a highly industrialised but small country with limited supplies of raw materials.

The main problem was the interaction of the raw materials deficit and the cumulative obstacles to foreign trade, in the course of Czechoslovakia's transition into East Europe's principal supplier of machinery (see p. 136). Increased consumption coupled with a shortage of high-quality raw materials led, on the one hand, to the utilisation of raw materials of inferior quality and, on the other hand, to the necessity to import essential high-quality raw materials from distant countries, which not only had to be paid for in convertible currency but also resulted in increased production costs. This forced Czechoslovakia to export at all costs; a factor which, in turn, reinforced the autarkic tendencies and worsened the terms of trade (see Tables 10.2 and 10.3).

As a result of this voluntary segregation from the Western markets, Czechoslovakia's exports of machinery to its Comecon trading partners soon reached a certain monopoly position. Consequently, there was a decline in the competitiveness of Czechoslovak industry in this sector, which also suffered from insufficient incentives for renewal and improvement within the central planning system. Step by step, this led to reductions in the quality of Czechoslovak products and to a relative technical backwardness, so that it became increasingly difficult to close the gap on the industrial nations of the West. According to the results of the official economic analyses conducted in the 1960s, in comparison with the international level of mechanical engineering products, only 36 per cent of Czechoslovak products met or exceeded the required standards; 27 per cent were obsolete and 37 per cent were in need of being replaced or scrapped. Hence, in many cases, it was only possible for Czechoslovakia to place its goods on the world market at a loss. Indeed, even in the Comecon countries, interest in Czechoslovak machinery began to wane from the middle of the 1950s. On the one hand, the output of their own industries had risen. On the other hand, they preferred to buy higher quality products from the West, which they could import again as the level of international tension relaxed after the Cold War. Furthermore, they were also interested in promoting the export of their own products which were becoming increasingly competitive with those of the ČSR in the world market. Thus the drastic restructuring of the country's foreign trade — as a result of the growing raw material and foreign trade barriers between 1948 and 1952 – led to a whole series of unfavourable

Table 10.2: Commodity structure of Czechoslovak foreign trade, 1949–80 (in foreign exchange kč millions and in %)

Commodity groups	E,I,B	1949 kč	1949 %	1953 kč	1953 %	1960 kč	1960 %
Total	E	5,805	100.0	7,153	100.0	13,892	100.0
	I	5,170	100.0	6,330	100.0	13,072	100.0
	B	635		823		820	
Machines, equipment	E	1,579	27.2	3,031	42.4	6,262	45.1
and tools	I	377	7.3	889	14.1	2,831	21.7
	B	1,202		2,142		3,431	
Fuels, raw materials	E	2,145	37.0	2,637	36.8	4,063	29.2
and minerals	I	3,342	64.6	3,433	54.2	6,935	53.0
	B	−1,197		−796		−2,872	
Breeding stock	E	6	0.1	1	0.0	15	0.1
and other animals	I	10	0.2	4	0.1	8	0.1
	B	−4		−3		7	
Foods including	E	455	7.8	613	8.6	722	5.2
raw materials	I	1,354	26.2	1,908	30.1	2,861	21.9
	B	−899		−1,295		−2,139	
Consumer goods	E	1,620	27.9	871	12.2	2,830	20.4
excluding foods	I	87	1.7	96	1.5	437	3.3
	B	1,533		775		2,393	
Finished goods — total	E					9,565	68.8
	I					4,690	36.0
	B					4,875	
Raw materials, fuel and	E					4,327	31.2
semi-finished goods,	I					8,382	64.0
including raw	B					−4,055	
materials for food							
production							

Note: E = Export, I = Import, B = Balance.
Source: *Statistická ročenka*, relevant years.

1965		1970		1975		1980	
kč	%	kč	%	kč	%	kč	%
19,357	100.0	27,305	100.0	46,651	100.0	80,163	100.0
19,242	100.0	26,605	100.0	50,176	100.0	81,540	100.0
115		700		−4,065		1,377	
9,385	48.5	13,712	50.2	22,404	48.0	40,227	50.2
5,758	29.9	8,871	33.3	18,707	36.9	29,844	36.6
3,627		4,841		3,697		10,383	
5,890	30.4	8,014	29.4	14,114	30.3	23,783	29.6
9,395	48.8	11,468	43.1	23,654	46.6	39,698	48.7
−3,505		−3,454		−9,540		−15,915	
34	0.2	25	0.1	49	0.1	59	0.1
24	0.2	69	0.3	42	0.1	78	0.1
10		−44		7		−19	
854	4.4	1,039	3.8	1,950	4.2	3,427	4.3
3,059	15.9	3,936	14.8	4,644	9.2	7.088	8.7
−2.205		−2,897		−2,694		−3,661	
3,194	16.5	4,515	16.5	8,134	17.4	12,667	15.8
1,006	5.2	2,261	8.5	3,669	7.2	4,832	5.9
2,188		2,254		4,465		7,835	
13,152	68.0	18,889	69.0	31,981	68.6	55,723	69.5
8,443	44.0	13,618	51.0	25,204	49.7	38,422	47.0
4,709		5,271		6,777		17,301	
6,205	32.0	8,416	31.0	14,670	31.4	24,440	30.5
10,799	56.0	12,987	49.0	25,512	50.3	43,118	53.0
−4,594		−4,571		−10,842		−18,678	

Table 10.3: Geographical distribution of Czechoslovak foreign trade, 1948–80 (in foreign exchange kč millions and in %)

	1948 kč	1948 %	1953 kč	1953 %	1960 kč	1960 %	1965 kč	1965 %	1970 kč	1970 %	1975 kč	1975 %	1980 kč	1980 %
Imports total from	4,904	100.0	6,328	100.0	13,072	100.0	19,242	100.0	26,605	100.0	50,716	100.0	81,540	100.0
socialist countries	1,949	39.7	4,992	78.9	9,316	71.3	14,121	73.4	18,462	69.4	35,398	70.0	57,214	70.2
non-socialist countries	2,955	60.3	1,336	21.1	3,756	28.7	5,121	26.6	8,143	30.6	15,318	30.0	24,326	29.8
Exports total to	5,429	100.0	7,153	100.0	13,892	100.0	19,357	100.0	27,305	100.0	46,651	100.0	80,163	100.0
socialist countries	2,149	39.6	5,587	78.1	10,041	72.3	14,151	73.1	19,288	70.6	33,377	71.6	55,799	69.6
non-socialist countries	3,280	60.4	1,566	21.9	3,851	27.7	5,206	26.9	8,017	29.4	13,274	28.4	24,364	30.4

Source: Databank of the Wiener Institut für Wirtschaftsvergleiche (calculated from relevant years of *Statistická ročenka*).

changes in the geographical direction and commodity distribution in Czechoslovakia's foreign trade with concomitant results on the structure of the economy.

Parallel to these changes, a barrier to consumption developed in the domestic market. Despite the fact that great successes had been recorded in the expansion of production capacities and in the level of industrial output, the division between the relative excess capacity of the producer goods industry and the slow growth on the consumer goods' side meant that the demands of the Czechoslovak population could not be satisfied. Whereas the respectable achievements in the fields of health care and education (see p. 129), as well as full employment, fulfilled the social expectations of the majority of citizens, they were, nevertheless, disappointed with their standard of living as expressed by personal consumption. In comparison with the consumer society developing in the West, the theory that centralised socialist planning would continuously increase the standard of living proved incompatible with the practice of maintaining barriers to consumption.

The growing shortage of workers in general and the lack of skilled craftsmen and women in particular formed a further barrier to growth. Under conditions of extensive economic development, not only material resources but also reserves of labour were mobilised and exhausted by the 1960s (see p. 150). In the investment plans, modernisation was not primarily expected to result in labour savings but in constant productivity improvements. The aim of the central planners was to achieve higher rates of growth in labour productivity rather than improved real rates of pay. Accordingly, wage rates were held within predetermined limits. With the exception of the reform period in the fourth five-year plan when the gap between productivity and wages began to close (see Table 9.1), this principle dominated in the long run. For example, in the years between 1955 and 1978, productivity increased by 41 per cent more than real wages. None the less, both labour productivity and the level of wages lagged markedly behind the levels attained in the Western industrial nations. This was due above all to the wages policy pursued by the central planning bodies with statutory wage catalogues reinforcing the levelling tendencies in Czechoslovak society. Furthermore, the practice of dictating either average wages or a predetermined wage fund left little room for financial incentives for the employees. All categories from managers to shop-floor workers were affected by this. This development took place within the framework of an unfavourable qualification and organisation structure which slowed down the process of technical innovation and renewal in the production process, as well as limiting productivity improvements. Accordingly, the efficiency of the labour input also suffered and this led to the scarcity of labour being emphasised as a barrier to economic growth.

During the second five-year plan (1955–60), Czechoslovakia received increased deliveries of raw materials from the Soviet Union to assist with the expansion of its heavy industry. Although this did not result in the elimination of imbalances, the shortage of raw materials was overcome and, at the end of the planning period, growth rates began to rise again. This prompted the party leadership to introduce the optimistic slogan: 'The attainment of socialism and the building of communism!' And President Novotný declared that, from 1960, Czechoslovakia would be known as the Czechoslovak Socialist Republic (ČSSR) (see p. 110).

The existing difficulties were regarded as deviations caused by excessive centralisation within the basically indisputable system of planning and control. The result was a first move in the direction of economic reform in 1958. However, these initial steps were aimed at improving, not changing the centrally controlled system. Particular emphasis was placed on industrial reorganisation, in order to make the individual enterprises more independent and to make them interested in performance and profit. Impetus in this direction was to be given by the reinforcement of the third level in the hierarchical planning pyramid in that the 24 main administration bodies responsible to the ministries were abolished and replaced with 383 production economic units (Výrobní hospodářská jednotka — VHJ). They were basically organised according to branches of industry, with each unit having its own budget independently of the ministries. These budgets were to be administered in accordance with economic criteria, that is, on the basis of cost benefit analysis. However, of the planned decentralisation only this organisational aspect survived because the financial reins were immediately tightened again by the central organs.

As the financial position worsened again, 1960 saw the start of a strong move in the direction of recentralisation. Officially, the small measures of reform were made responsible for the negative signs in economic growth. However, these measures had in no way touched the basic concept of the planning system, which continued to worsen the imbalances in the Czechoslovak economy.

In the field of foreign policy, the Sino-Soviet conflict and the consequent abrupt breach of trade relations with China had a particularly unfavourable impact on Czechoslovak industry, which had taken on large orders and was left with more products to add to the existing stocks of unsaleable goods. At the same time, the supply of foodstuffs from China also dried up, so that Czechoslovakia suddenly had to import large quantities at world-market prices. In turn, this resulted in a worsening of the country's balance of trade and payments.

The fundamentally erroneous asumption made by the planners — that a continuous increase in gross capital investment and the output of producer goods is consummate with an efficient economy — first became apparent as it proved impossible to meet even the initial demands of the third five-year plan (1961–5) and it had to be abandoned after the first year. The centrally administered planned economy was not capable of co-ordinating the processes of economic life. This was reflected in the economic crisis of 1961–3 which, although it affected all Comecon countries in the form of declining economic growth, reached its nadir in the Czechoslovak economy with negative growth rates.

ON THE WAY TO REFORMING THE PLANNING SYSTEM (1964–8)

Prematurely ended, the unsuccessful reform of 1958/9 and the — officially impossible but none the less real — collapse of Czechoslovakia's planned socialist economy not only gave rise to widespread dissatisfaction in general but also led to increasing criticism of the economy and system of control at all levels of the KSČ. Among the communist intelligentsia in particular, people began to make critical analyses of the economic, socio-political, technical-scientific and cultural conditions. This is where the roots of the reform movement are to be found. Characteristic of this movement is the fact that it developed within the party itself and, therefore, was able to spread its influence gradually to the central leadership. While the authoritarian system continued in existence, the Communist Party was subjected to a process of democratisation from within, the aim of which was to criticise the economic and political structure which the party itself had created and, through fundamental reforms, to develop a socialist economy in a political democracy based on socialism. In the history of the various reform movements in the Comecon countries, Czechoslovakia was the first country where economic and political change was demanded simultaneously from within and without the Communist Party. And considering Czechoslovakia's long democratic tradition and its relatively advanced economic level, the chances of success were better than in other parts of Central and Southeast Europe.

The doors permitting the reformers to exercise increased influence were opened by the Central Committee of the KSČ at the end of 1962, when commissions and working groups were charged with preparing 'basic principles for perfecting the centrally administered planning system'. Antonín Novotný, the President of the Republic and First Secretary of the KSČ, appointed the Director of the Institute of Economics of the Czechoslovak Academy of Sciences, Ota Šik, a member of the Central Committee of the KSČ with whom he had been together in a concentration camp and who enjoyed his complete trust, as head of the Commission of Economic Experts. In September 1964 the KSČ proposals were put forward as a draft plan for 'restructuring the economic system' based on the results of academic research. The overall system of administrative and centrally directed planning and control was made fundamentally responsible for the country's economic problems. Accordingly, all attempts to improve the old system were rejected on principle and change demanded through the application of scientific planning methods with a broader utilisation of the market mechanism. The reform-orientated groups succeeded in convincing the Central Committee of the KSČ of this and the changes were introduced with a resolution concerning the 'main directions for the perfection of the centrally planned economy and the work of the party' in January 1965. The start of the progressive transition to a socialist planned and market economy has its roots in the directives for the fourth five-year plan (1966–70), between April and October 1966. The basic principles of this economic reform may be summarised as follows: because socialist property relations dominated in all sectors of the Czechoslovak economy, the economic reformers built on the basis of state ownership of the means of production. The economy was to continue to be guided by central development plans and, at the same time, measures were to be taken to reduce the degree of bureaucracy and decentralise the planning system with planning autonomy for enterprises in all economic sectors, except banking, on the basis of business profitability accounting. The market mechanism was to be incorporated in the control of the individual economic processes.

The justification for the inclusion of market forces in the planned economy was explained and discussed at all levels of the party, in all factories and offices, as well as in all mass organisations such as the trade unions and youth movement. In the mid-1960s, a contradictory situation developed in which a continuous and widespread discussion, about the causes of the country's economic failures and how mistakes in the planning system could be brought to light and corrected in the future, took place openly despite the existence of authoritarian political conditions. This discussion met with a positive response among the population at large and gradually gained acceptance among the trade unions, which had been the handmaids of the party and central planning bodies since 1948. In this way, the general public came to accept that introducing the restructured economic system, as well as overcoming the faults and realising the symbiosis of market and plan, would be a long and painful process.

The turbulent years from 1965 to 1968 were decisive for the development of the economic reform. To provide a scientific foundation for the political decision-making process, research groups and, above all, the Czechoslovak Academy of Sciences not only investigated structural changes in the economy but also in social stratification as well as the legal system. A broadly based interdisciplinary team of approximately 60 academics under the leadership of Radovan Richta attempted a comprehensive evaluation of social change under the impact of the scientific and technical revolution. Although many of the research results which appeared in pioneering publications never found practical application, they aroused general interest and the knowledge contained in them has not lost its great historical significance. On the one hand, the process of democratisation in the Czechoslovak Communist Party permitted the blossoming of previously repressed initiatives among the rank-and-file party members, as well as among the non-communist citizens in general. These movements increasingly pressed for the theoretical socialist and democratic principles of the constitution, the legal system, the voting system to be implemented in the state, in the party, in the trade unions and other social organisations, and for action to be taken to eliminate the crass difference between theory and practice. On the other hand, every new regulation made to realise the reforms met with determined resistance from the bureaucratic apparatuses of the party and the state which clung wherever possible to the directive commands and familiar methods of administrative control and only gave in reluctantly to pressure to accelerate the reform process. Pulling in opposite directions, these contrary endeavours were reflected in the transition to the new planning and control system.

The first major intervention in 1965 led to a change in the 'organisational structure of the productive and technical base'. The production economic units (VHJ) created in 1958 were retained but they were amalgamated in trusts according to branches of industry and thereby reduced to 99 in number (see p. 148). The management of the VHJ was handed over to specialist managing boards. The personnel of these boards was to be selected from competent employees who were to be trained in accordance with modern business and production methods. For this purpose, a research and teaching institute for business management which organised one-year courses for top managers was set up in Prague in 1965. The intention was that the new trusts should lead to specialisation and the elimination of the numerous industry ministries. However, this aim was not achieved due to the brakes being applied 'from above'. In contradistinction to the ideas of the reformers, the tips of the hierarchical pyramids were reinforced by the firmly established concentration of the trusts, whereas, instead of becoming more independent, in many cases the enterprises subordinated to them continued to be bureaucratically manipulated.

Nevertheless, with the introduction of the new economic system based on the principle of 'central planning of the economy with decentralised planning of the economic processes', the decentralising tendencies started to loosen the foundation stones of the centralised system of control. Thus, in the Government Decree of 12 December 1966, the enterprises were no longer given obligatory tasks but were expected to orient their economic development in accordance with the recommended plan targets. Material interest in business success was also stimulated with the introduction of the so-called 'gross-income principle'. Equal financial commitments to the state were created through the imposition of standard taxes. This meant that, after deduction of these basic dues — a 6 per cent 'basic means' tax, a 2 per cent 'assets' tax and an 18 per cent 'stabilisation' tax on their gross income — the individual enterprises could dispose freely of the remaining, net income. This distribution policy gave the enterprises greater freedom in the financing of investments from their own resources and permitted a more elastic wage policy, although certain measures were also introduced at the same time to prevent the payment of exaggerated wage increases and premiums. In consideration of the labour shortage, enterprises with a disproportionate number of workers had to reckon with a 'total wage' tax. In the long run, it was thought that supply and demand would determine the participation of all workers in the relative success of their enterprises and, consequently, there would be a 'de-levelling' of income, as well as an increase in labour productivity and economic efficiency.

In 1966, attaining planned targets was also simplified for the Unified Agricultural Co-operatives (JZD) by permitting them to make contracts setting out the quantities and composition of their deliveries with the state purchasing offices. This expanded their room for manoeuvre, not to mention their material interest in increasing production. At the same time, the state purchasing prices for agricultural products were increased more than the prices of farm machinery and other means of production. The end effect was that co-operatives and their individual members were not only able to earn bigger profits and higher incomes but also to mechanise their farms to a greater extent from their own resources, as well as employ bio-technical and chemical products. Even before the end of the fourth five-year plan, these benefits led to the use of improved methods of cultivation and livestock breeding and, in the long term, to a more balanced supply of food for the population and had a favourable impact on national income and the trade balance.

The investment policy was of fundamental significance for the new system of control. In all sectors of the economy, enterprises were given greater decision-making freedom in respect of investments made from their own resources. On the part of the central planners, investment decisions were made with the aim of relieving the pressure of capital spending in the producer goods industries and reducing the existing disproportions and out-of-balance forces. Although the volume of funds flowing into heavy industry remained relatively high, large proportions of its output were allocated for equipping light industry, with the wood, paper, clothing and building materials industries benefiting in particular. A change in the overall pattern of investment was starting to take place in favour of the consumer goods industries (see p. 160). On the one hand, this served to raise consumer satisfaction in the domestic market and, on the other hand, to expand the production volume of competitive finished goods for export.

Because the reactivation of free-market relationships in the new system of control required a more realistic price system, it was necessary for officially fixed prices to give way to free-market prices, in the sense of decentralised planning of the economic process. There were fears, however, that complete abolishment of price controls in the sellers' market existing at that time would lead to inflationary developments. In order to avoid this, the price reform was introduced in two phases: the first affected wholesale prices only; in the second phase, prices were to be predominantly set by the free interaction of market forces.

In the first phase, during 1966, wholesale prices were determined on the basis of costs, as well as supply and demand criteria, using electronic data processing equipment and introduced in three categories from 1 January 1967. The first category set fixed prices for 15 per cent of production goods such as important raw materials, fuels and energy, as well as for more than 75 per cent of all consumer goods, mainly basic foodstuffs. The second category set limit prices for 80 per cent of all producer goods, while the third category permitted free prices for 5 per cent of producer goods and 20 per cent of consumer goods, for example, luxury products and services. The results of this first phase did not correspond with the enormous effort involved in the price revision, because the fixed-price system meant that no significant changes took place in the market. Due to the continuous pressure of demand for producer goods, their prices remained at the upper limit and the free prices rose more than expected. The result was that the enterprises recorded oversized net profits which, in turn, gave rise to inflationary pressures.

In the second phase, which began in the summer of 1967, modifications were made to the pricing system, the number of limited prices increased considerably and the previous distinction between wholesale and retail prices was bridged over by a standard sales tax. The prices of approximately half of all products on both levels were to have been freed by 1969 and in this way assistance given to the expansion of free-market conditions.

The step-by-step deregulation of prices and the recreation of a relationship between wholesale and retail prices also contributed to the planned reduction of the gap between domestic and world price levels. In the reform, this was considered to be an important prerequisite of the planned liberalisation and, later, for full convertibility of the Czechoslovak crown. In this way, the reformers tried to end the isolation of the ČSSR from the world market. On an organisational plane, the new system weakened the foreign-trade monopoly of the ministry by entitling domestic enterprises and specialist foreign-trade agents to operate directly in appropriate world markets. It was hoped that the competitive pressure of world trade would force Czechoslovak enterprises to introduce technical improvements. Through working of the market mechanism, changes in the territorial distribution and commodity composition exports were to bring the pattern of Czechoslovak foreign trade more into line with its traditional role. By the beginning of the 1970s Czechoslovakia succeeded in increasing the value of its exports of finished products to a level in excess of its imports of fuels and raw materials and in this way achieved an active balance of trade. In respect of the territorial distribution, an increasing share of the country's foreign trade was aimed at the Western industrial nations and developing countries with convertible currencies. However, the foreign-trade reform also took into account the special position of the Soviet Union and the Comecon countries because, since being restructured in the 1950s, the range of Czechoslovak exports was more likely to find buyers in these markets than in the free world markets (see Table 10.3). Because, in accordance with Comecon decisions, prices had been set on the basis of the average of world prices of the preceding five years since 1958, and because the Comecon prices for 1965/6 were based on average world-market prices from 1960 to 1964, the reform included this in its planning. That is to say, the Comecon price level was to act on domestic prices in the ČSSR in a similar way to world-market prices. Thus, the principle of price adjustment was to be applied to all of Czechoslovakia's foreign-trade partners.

In the course of the expansion of the new economic system, the introduction of new regulations and measures was obstructed by delays and resistance in the central organs. Dissatisfaction with the slow progress of the reform and bureaucratic resistance to the planned process of democratisation became widespread. During 1967, the role of Slovakia — in particular, that of the national question which had been building up for some time — shifted into the forefront. The reformers considered it essential to regulate finally the relationship of the Czech and Slovak regions on a federal basis, within the framework of a general solution to the nationalities problems in the republic. In Slovakia, there had been a build-up of resentment, with the 'asymmetric system' of Czech–Slovak relations causing particular bitterness. This regulation meant that the smaller population in Slovakia represented one-third of the state and led to the Czech majority dominating the Slovak minority in the central organs. Among Slovaks, this reinforced the conviction that Slovak interests were necessarily being neglected as all decisions were taken in Prague.

In the centralist and authoritarian régime, the 'Slovak question' had been basically reduced to overcoming the minority's relative economic backwardness through accelerated industrialisation, a concept which fitted neatly into the overall planning system. And, without doubt, a dramatic process of industrialisation did take place in Slovakia. The rate of growth of the region's industrial output rose annually by approximately 13 per cent between 1948 and 1968, thus exceeding the growth rates of the Czech part as well as that of total industrial production. Although this gave a considerable boost to schooling, education and culture in Slovakia, industrial developments in this part of Czechoslovakia took place without taking account of the overall national and regional economic needs of the country. At the same time as the generally unsatisfactory consequences of the centrally administered system of control were being felt in Slovakia, there was also a basic weakness consisting of the ineffectiveness of the new large-scale industrial enterprises, which had been constructed at great cost over an inordinate length of time: not only was their technical standard too low but they were neither an integrated whole nor a harmonious part of the Slovak economy. Although theoretically on an equal footing, in the sense of the bureaucratic and mechanistic approach of the regime, Slovakia also had to accept only a third of the total in the distribution of financial resources. Hence, it was the relative economic and political neglect of Slovakia which was considered to be the main injustice and, within the reform movement, the realisation of a federal solution to the national question became the primary Slovak demand.

As the reform gathered momentum, it became evident that the new economic instruments, which were based on the interaction of plan and market, were incompatible with the continuation of the centralised bureaucratic planning system within the party and state apparatuses. The links between economics and politics became increasingly obvious and it soon became apparent that the authoritarian political system was the main obstacle in the way of complete implementation of the economic reforms. This situation resulted in a political struggle within the Central Committee of the Czechoslovak Communist Party which, in January 1968, came to a head with the displacement of Antonín Novotný and his replacement as First Secretary of the Central Committee of the KSČ by the former Slovak party secretary, Alexander Dubček. On 30 March 1968 General Ludvík Svoboda was elected President of the ČSSR by the National Assembly.

With his sincere manner and honest endeavours to bring about a political framework for the creation of improved living conditions under 'socialism with a human face', Dubček soon gained the confidence of the population. Under his leadership, the decision-making processes in the party and the state were transferred to the reform-orientated group of the Central Committee of the KSČ, which had majority backing. The economic reform was given a decisive boost with the 'Action Programme' approved at the plenary meeting of the Central Committee of the KSČ on 5 April 1968. This is also reflected in the fact that in the same month Ota Šik, the Chairman of the Government Commission for Economic Reform, was elected Deputy Prime Minister of Czechoslovakia.

Despite the increasing number of threats coming from the

Soviet Union (Brezhnev), the GDR (Ulbricht) and Poland (Gomulka), the spring and summer of 1968 — known as the 'Prague Spring' — were characterised by popular enthusiasm for the introduction of reforms, as well as much optimism for the future. Although not a great deal was achieved by way of a reform of the individual processes in the micro-economic sphere during these months, the monopoly of power and opinion held by the Communist Party was subjected to a process of democratisation. In order to promote the independence of the enterprises in everyday business life, the party organs were instructed to confine themselves to matters connected with the framework of planning and not to relieve the managers of state and co-operative enterprises of their responsibility through constant administrative and supervisory interference. The democratisation of the managing bodies of these enterprises began in April 1968 with the spontaneous formation of works councils which, in response to pressure 'from below', were included in the party and trade-union programme for the realisation of the principle of co-determination. The trade unions began to give some thought to their independent role as the representatives of the interests of their members in relation to the works management. In the trade unions, as well as at all levels of the party organisation, new elections were held without the restricting guidance of the party apparatus. This was an extremely important step for the release of democratic forces within the framework of the preparations for the XIV Party Congress — and the election of a new Central Committee of the KSČ scheduled for 9 September 1968.

Programmatic reports were prepared for consideration at the planned Party Congress; above all the 'Action Programme of the Communist Party of Czechoslovakia' mentioned above, the 'Draft Concept for the Further Development of the Directed Economic System' (also known as the '77 Point Programme') of June 1968 and the 'Guidelines for the Economy in 1969', published just a few days before the invasion of the country. These documents contained both a brief historical analysis of the causes of the social and economic crisis and a critical inventory of the 'New Type of Five-Year Plan' introduced in 1966, as well as special guidelines for the future course to be taken by Czechoslovakia's economy and society on the way to socialism. Three main aims are evident from them. First, the basic principles of socialism were to be adhered to. Secondly, the reform that had been started was to be implemented un-compromisingly and the economy made to function efficiently. And, thirdly, that this could only be achieved through the creation of a democratic political system. Although the overall concept for the new economic system had been worked out and a start made on its introduction by August, 1968, the Soviet-led invasion of Czechoslovakia by Warsaw Pact troops on 21 August 1968 prevented the Party Congress of the KSČ being held and put an abrupt end to all democratisation plans.

'NORMALISATION' OF THE CENTRALLY ADMINISTERED AND DIRECTIVE SYSTEM OF ECONOMIC PLANNING AND CONTROL (1969–80)

Together with all members of the Politburo, Alexander Dubček was abducted to Moscow in the same night as the Warsaw Pact troops arrived in Europe, on 20/21 August. Although the Soviet government asserted that they had been asked for assistance by Czechoslovak communists, nobody was prepared to confirm this. On the contrary, so great was the outrage of the entire population of Czechoslovakia at the military invasion by their allies, so great was their conviction that — as in Munich in 1938 — they had been betrayed, and so vehement was their reaction to this act of aggression, that the President of the Republic, Ludvík Svoboda, flew to Moscow to plead for the release of the imprisoned politicians with the result that, on 27 August, the party leadership was flown back to Prague unharmed. With the massive support of the people and, in particular, from the indignant trade unions, Dubček held on as First Secretary of the Czechoslovak Communist Party for some months. His position, however, was rapidly undermined by the pressure of the occupation and the increased number of Soviet advisors in political and economic life, by the displacement of reformers, as well as by the more and more prevalent atmosphere of disappointment and indifference among the population. In April 1969 Gustav Husák took over the leadership of the KSČ and later, after the death of Ludvík Svoboda, the presidency of the republic, too. Husák belonged to those who had been convicted in the 'bourgeois nationalists' show trials in the 1950s and rehabilitated in the early 1960s. After returning to political life he became a member of the Central Committee of the KSČ, where he worked for greater autonomy for Slovakia. During the reform period, he was made Deputy Prime Minister. Nevertheless, after the invasion, he soon came to terms with the Brezhnev policy and became the leading figure of the 'process of normalisation' in Czechoslovakia.

The main objective of the Soviet government, as well as the dogmatic members of the KSČ leadership who were back on the ascent, was to undo the political reforms without delay. Although the political attitudes of the initiators and the proponents of the economic reform were damned as a betrayal of the socialist system, the influence of those revisions to the planning and directive system which had already been implemented was felt until into the early 1970s. This is reflected in the growth rates of all indicators (see Table 9.1B): particularly beneficial proved to be the improved economic balance between the production of consumer and producer goods which, coupled with increasing productivity, resulted in higher wages and an improved level of consumption for the population.

As the only aim of the reform movement to be completely fulfilled, the federalisation of the two parts of Czechoslovakia made history by putting their administration on an equal footing. As from 1 January 1969 the ČSSR was made up of two 'symmetric', autonomous states: The Czech Socialist Republic (ČSR) and the Slovak Socialist Republic (SSR). The middle of 1969, however, marked the beginning of the definitive return to the pre-reform situation in an atmosphere of political pressure with 'cleansing' measures and retaliatory actions being followed by mass expulsions from the KSČ, numerous dismissals and transfers, especially among intellectuals. Many people emigrated, many more were prohibited from going about their work. In the economy, social-market principles became taboo and there was a sharp move back towards centralisation. However, the results of the economic reform were not completely negated.

The de-control of prices on a limited number of goods and services had resulted in a slightly inflationary tendency: between 1 January and 31 December 1968 the price level rose by 2.4 per cent. With the confusion caused by the invasion at the end of August 1968 there was a further increase in inflationary pressure as people withdrew their savings and made panic purchases. In May 1969, in order to restrict consumption, the government ordered all retail prices to be increased, with the exception of basic foodstuffs which only rose by 0.7 per cent. On 2 July 1969 all prices were frozen and central price controls successively reintroduced. According to official statistics, prices rose by an average of 5.3 per cent between 1 January and 31 December 1969. The prices of consumer durables went up by 9 per cent: among them, shoes and leather products by 11 per cent and household goods by 22 per cent. At the same time, strict wage controls were reintroduced to regulate increases in incomes.

Particularly high priority in the process of 'normalisation' was given to the election and functioning of works councils, an institution which had spread to many enterprises. In May 1969 the creation of new works councils was forbidden. Soon after the existing works councils were dissolved. Step by step, there was a return to the centrally administered and directed system of control with obligatory plan targets in physical units. In the micro-economic sphere, enterprises were once again bound to detailed plans. As in the pre-reform years, these methods favoured industrial operations working with high production costs at the cost of efficiently run enterprises. Agricultural undertakings were merged into large units. Foreign trade was also brought back into the centrally directed planning system, although some companies were permitted to continue operating directly in the world market.

In the course of the normalisation process, the old long-term trends reasserted themselves within the framework of Czechoslovakia's planned economy. Once again, barriers to growth became increasingly evident. Table 9.1B shows the reduction in the rate of growth of the main indicators. Although less than the 6.9 per cent of the reform period, the rate of growth of national income amounted to a still respectable 5.7 per cent during the first half of the 1970s. It was not until the sixth five-year plan from 1975 to 1980 that the growth rate dropped to 3.7 per cent (and to 2.6 per cent in 1980), that is, to the lowest level since the crisis of 1960–65. In terms of industrial production, too, growth rates were on the decline: from 6.7 per cent in 1965–70 to 5 per cent in 1975–80. In this case, however, the previous imbalances started to become more and more apparent: while the rate of growth in the producer goods sector fell by only 1.1 percentage points (from 7.2 to 6.1 per cent), the production of consumer goods fell by no less than 5.3 percentage points (from 7.9 to 2.6 per cent). An attendant phenomenon of this return to the old system of priorities was the significant slowing down in the rate of growth of average wages from 5.4 per cent to 1.2 per cent and in personal consumption from 5.4 per cent to 2.6 per cent, the lowest growth rates since 1948 (see Table 9.1B).

The increasing difficulties faced by the Czechoslovak economy in the years up to 1980 were primarily due to the return to the old planning concept with its emphasis on heavy industry, as well as the reintroduction of the inflexible system of centrally directed planning and control. In addition, the economic situation of the ČSSR was negatively influenced by external factors, in particular the international energy crisis which accentuated the existing shortage of fuel and power.

This is also the reason for the decision of the other Comecon countries that Czechoslovakia should increase its production of fuels, energy and semi-finished metal products, as well as machinery for nuclear power stations and electricity works: a decision which necessarily reinforced the imbalance in the economic structure of the ČSSR, because every increase in industrial production required a higher level of investment than in the past. At the same time, there was a sharp turn in the terms of trade against Czechoslovakia. Since 1973 the Czechoslovak balance of payments has registered an increasing deficit (from US$80 million in 1973 to US$1,128.3 million in 1979). At the end of the 1970s imports of energy and raw materials — for which higher prices had to be paid — reached 50 per cent of total imports while 70 per cent of total exports consisted of industrial products — the prices of which fell relatively on the world market. The deficit caused by the import of fuels and raw materials could no longer be balanced out by the export of finished goods (see Table 10.2).

The unfavourable development of the terms of trade in the second half of the 1970s not only led to a significant increase in Czechoslovakia's trade deficit with Western industrial nations but also to a marked deterioration of its trading position with the other Comecon countries and a passive balance of trade with the USSR. Only in the case of trade with developing countries did the Czechoslovak balance of trade remain active. Although the surpluses were in convertible currency and, theoretically, could have been freely disposed of, problems arose because these exports had been financed with long-term credits.

In the post-reform period, the room for manoeuvre available to the Czechoslovak economy was greatly restricted by a variety of internal and external factors. A fundamental economic reform hardly falls in the realm of realistic possibilities in the foreseeable future, so that the country's firm bonds to the Soviet Union will remain of vital importance to the Czechoslovak economy. These links guarantee the supply of the indispensable fuels and raw materials, as well as a market for a large proportion of Czechoslovak products. The development of the centrally directed and administered system of planning and control in the years after the invasion up to 1980 reflects the process of 'normalisation', in other words, the adherence to and the consolidation of the pre-reform line.

Select Bibliography

ECONOMIC HISTORY

Very few publications deal with the economic and social history of Czechoslovakia from the country's establishment as an independent state in 1918 to the present. The following is a survey of the socioeconomic development from 1918 to 1968:

Průcha, V. *et al* (eds), *Hospodářské dějiny Československa v 19. a 20. století* (The economic history of Czechoslovakia in the nineteenth and twentieth centuries), Prague, 1974.

The economic history of Slovakia is contained in:

Faltus, J. and V. Průcha, (eds), *Prehľad hospodárskeho vývoja na Slovensku v rokoch 1918–1945* (Survey of the economic development in Slovakia during the years from 1918 to 1945), Bratislava, 1969.

Czechoslovakia is included in:

Kaser, M.C. and E.A. Radice (eds), *The economic history of Eastern Europe 1919–1975.* vol. I: *Economic structure and performance between the two wars*, Oxford, 1985; vol. II: *Interwar policy, the war and reconstruction*, Oxford, 1986; vol. III: *Institutional change within a planned economy*, Oxford, 1986.

For problems of Czechoslovakia as part of the international economy, see:

Teichova, A., *An economic background to Munich. International business and Czechoslovakia 1918–1938*, Cambridge, 1974.

ASPECTS OF THE ECONOMIC AND SOCIAL HISTORY OF CZECHOSLOVAKIA

1918–1945

Faltus, J., *Povojnová hospodárska kríza v Československu v rokoch 1921–1923* (The postwar economic crisis in Czechoslovakia 1921–1923), Bratislava, 1966.

Hájek, M., *Od Mnichova k 15.3.1939* (From Munich to the 15 March 1939), Prague, 1959.

Král, V., *Otázky hospodářského a sociálního vývoje v českých zemích v letech 1938–1945* (Problems of economic and social development in the Czech Lands in the years 1938–1945), 3 vols., Prague, 1957–9.

Krejčí, J., 'Volkseinkommenvergleich Österreich-ČSR', in *Beiträge zur Wirtschaftspolitik und Wirtschaftswissenschaft* II, Vienna, n.d.

164

Lacina, V., 'K dynamice hospodářského vývoje v předmnichovské ČSR' (The dynamism of economic development in the pre-Munich ČSR), in *Sborník historický* 23 (1976).

Lacina, V., 'K místu Československa v evropské a světové ekonomice v letech 1918–1938' (The place of Czechoslovakia in the world economy 1918–1938), in *Československý časopis historický* 26 (1976).

Lacina, V., *Velká hospodářská krise v Československu 1929–1934* (The great economic crisis in Czechoslovakia 1929–1934), Prague, 1984.

Pryor, F.L., Z.P. Pryor, M. Stádník and J.G. Staller, 'Czechoslovak aggregate production in the interwar period', in *Review of Income and Wealth* 17 (1971).

Pryor, Z.P. and F.L. Pryor, 'Foreign trade and interwar Czechoslovak economic development 1918–1938', in *Vierteljahrschrift für Sozial- und Wirtschaftsgeschichte* 62 (1975).

Pryor, Z.P., 'Czechoslovak fiscal policies in the Great Depression', in *Economic History Review* 29 (1976).

Teichova, A. and P.L. Cottrell (eds), *International business and Central Europe 1918–1939*, Leicester, New York, 1983.

Teichova, A., 'A comparative view of the inflation of the 1920s in Austria and Czechoslovakia', in Schmukler, N. and E. Marcus (eds), *Inflation through the ages: economic, social, psychological and historical aspects*, New York, 1983.

1945–80

Adam, J., *Wage, price and taxation policy in Czechoslovakia 1948–1970*, Berlin, 1974.

Altmann, F.L. and J. Sláma, *Strukturentwicklung der tschechoslowakischen Wirtschaft und ihre Rückwirkung auf den Außenhandel*, Osteuropa-Institut, München, 1976.

Bloomfield, J., *Passive revolution, politics and the Czechoslovak working class 1945–1948*, London, 1979.

Goldmann, J. and K. Kouba, *Economic growth in Czechoslovakia*, Prague, 1969.

Hensel, K.P. *et al.*, *Die sozialistische Marktwirtschaft der Tschechoslowakei*, Stuttgart, 1968.

Kořalka, J., 'Tchecoslovaquie. Les pays Tcheques. Small enterprises in the economic and social life of the Czech Lands, 1848–1979' in: *Petite entreprise et croissance industrielle dans le monde aux XIXᵉ et XXᵉ siècles*, Editions du Centre National de la Recherche Scientifique, Paris, 1981, Vol. II, 666–705.

Kosta, J., *Abriss der sozioökonomischen Entwicklung der Tschechoslowakei 1945–1977*, Frankfurt-am-Main, 1978.

Krejčí, J., 'Vývoj československého hospodářství v globální analýze' (The development of the Czechoslovak economy in global analysis), in *Politická ekonomie* 6 (1968).

Krejčí, J., 'Intertemporal comparability of national income in Czechoslovakia', in *Review of Income and Wealth* 3 (1968).

Krejčí, J., *Social change and stratification in postwar Czechoslovakia*, London, 1972.
Krejčí, J., *National income and outlay in Czechoslovakia, Poland and Yugoslavia*, London, 1982.
Levcik, F., *Czechoslovakia: economic performance in the post-reform period and prospects for the 1980s. East European economic assessment*, Part I, Country Studies 1980, Washington, DC, 1981.
Myant, M., *Socialism and democracy in Czechoslovakia 1945–1948*, Cambridge, 1981.
Machonin, P. et al., *Československá společnost* (Czechoslovak society), Prague, 1969.
Šik, O., *Czechoslovakia: the bureaucratic economy*, White Plains, NY, 1972, Vienna, Munich, Zurich, 1969.
Šik, O., *Plan and market under socialism*, Prague, 1967.
Sláma, J., *Die sozio-ökonomische Umgestaltung der Nachkriegs-Tschechoslowakei*, Wiesbaden, 1977.

ASPECTS OF THE POLITICAL HISTORY OF CZECHOSLOVAKIA

Hoensch, J.K., *Geschichte der Tschechoslowakischen Republik 1918–1948*, Stuttgart, 1978.
Liptak, L., *Slovensko v 20. storočí* (Slovakia in the twentieth century), Bratislava, 1968.
Mamatey, V.S. and R. Luža (eds), *A History of the Czechoslovak Republic 1918–1948*, Princeton, 1973.
Olivová, V., *The doomed democracy, Czechoslovakia in a disrupted Europe 1914–1938*, London, 1972.
Seton-Watson, R.W., *A history of Czechs and Slovaks*, Hamden, 1965.
Wallace, W.W., *Czechoslovakia*, London, 1977.

NATIONAL AND INTERNATIONAL ASPECTS OF CZECHOSLOVAK HISTORY

Bosl, K. (ed.), *Die Erste Tschechoslowakische Republik als ein multinationaler Parteienstaat*, Munich, Vienna, 1979.
Bosl, K. (ed.), *Gleichgewicht = Revision = Restauration. Die Aussen-politik der Ersten Tschechoslowakischen Republik im Europasystem der Pariser Vorortverträge*, Munich, 1976.
Brügel, J.W., *Tschechen und Deutsche 1918–1938*, Munich, 1967.
Brügel, J.W., *Tschechen und Deutsche 1939–1946*, Munich, 1974.
Janeček, O. et al., *Odboj a revoluce 1938–1945. Nástin dějín československého odboje* (Resistance and revolution 1938–1945. Outline history of the Czechoslovak resistance), Prague, 1965.
Luža, R., *The transfer of the Sudeten Germans: a study of Czech–German relations 1933–1962*, New York, London, 1964.
Richta, R., et al., *Civilization at the crossroads: social and human implications of the scientific and technical revolution*, trans. M. Šlingová, 3rd expanded edn, Prague, 1969.

Index